Hinterland Rose

Elizabeth Clayton

Hinterland Rose

Copyright © 2023 Elizabeth Clayton

Library of Congress Control Number: 2023936463
                    Paperback: 978-1-960362-90-2
                    eBook: 978-1-960362-91-9

Hinterland Rose

The rose is the epitome of the
flower, its blossom the
metaphor of remembrance,
keeping with the first, and the last.
And the flower is, philosophically,
the spokeswoman of all beauty, as the grail,
patterning the all good, our efforts toward, ever,
the intrinsic good –
our goal, conscious or unaware, with all
effort or less –
And in accomplishing the grail, we do not,
as becoming, in itself, realize the rose,
for every endeavor toward becoming
cannot, in these realms, become a rose;
it is, however, within the endeavoring, the striving,
the pressing that lies,
in small or larger part,
the objectively real,
the become, the lovely rose.

Elizabeth
October 16, 2019

The rose is conceived in darkness, to open full,
in light's supremacy.

A crown is but the open flower in sunshine's bright.

A Note to My Readers

In my earliest memories of writing, especially in cursive or script, I was taught to form a worthy central idea, a thesis sentence, to then organize supporting material, choose appropriate transitional elements and present the entire composition with as few grammatical errors as possible.

Through the following years, these instructions helped me fare well, even into graduate school, especially into graduate school, of which I chose two fields of study: English Literature and Psychology. Many compositions were required, throughout, and when I began to write for publication, in 2007, my lessons were still in place.

Through these twelve – thirteen years, and twenty-three works, primarily poetry, I find some departure from my original pattern, not because of its lack of merit, but circumstances in my life which have called on me to reach my writing goals in a somewhat different fashion.

In 1965, I was diagnosed with Bipolar I, and nearly ten years ago the full press of Rheumatoid Arthritis impinged on my body and psyche, a most negative factor being in the medication arena. I continued to write, with a will and passion, as my mania, not nearly always controlled, insisted, but I began to choose alternate routes to achieve my, then, metamorphosing goals. Anxiety attacks were common, lethargy and depression, and great fatigue were always present, as was depersonalization. The problem of balance, with motivation, made almost all future goals difficult ventures. And then, as an apparent coup to my remaining sanity, two years ago I began a two-year bout with grave hallucinogenic symptoms. There were no case histories, to speak of, nor any pointing to a medication that would hold me; everything from dementia to Parkinson's related dementia, were suggested; with a guess of psychotropic medications, the images finally went away, and have returned only as some, more, hypnogogic imagery.

I continued to write, as a cathartic measure, at times slipping back into older styles and themes, but more, my poetry has become darker, courting the subject of conclusion, and colored by doubt, pushing me to an agonizing prayer life, for respite, if not repose. My hold was tenuous, and I knew, so, my becoming reclusive and silent, vocally. But solitude is sweet balm; andso I come to say the verse describing where my thoughts have come to wander; I am not so well and organized, and my transitions, often times, are somewhat poor maneuvers – but true to my thought, aware, and processing. The work is, in reality, a lengthy introduction\preface and six small books of supporting verse, always written in free verse.

And as the theme is concluded, all thought that is strong enough, true enough,
and lovely – becomes the rose which has journeyed out its hinterlands.

Elizabeth
January 20, 2020
At twilight

The Limber lost

Originally a 13,000-acre swamp in eastern Indiana, this area became host to early twentieth century, American novelist and naturalist, Gene Stratton-Porter. The limber lost is a beautiful, natural work of appearance and reality. Dark, wet, and dangerous, it now, having been modified, also easily offers glorious color and form in nature's live sculptures: birds, butterflies, and moths of most pristine varieties, with reptiles, fish, and other water creatures. These live together in a harmony that allows, perchance, the proverbial home in forever, under the smile of giant fern and grasses, radiant lily and medicinal varieties of bells and berries. Resting against trees of every description, canes spring out peeling, and such – all umbrellaed by the mercurial brilliant sun, the demurely casting moon.

The Moth and the Flame

The moth is so arranged, engineered, that it finds its distance and angels in flight from sources of light, but it is fascinated by the brightness of the light, wishing to attend, commune with it, indeed, perishing in its flame – the truth in a paradox – the complete language of living. As beauty and good are our need, our very bright, ought to do in fully communing is to offer up our whole selves in physical death, that we then be part and real in whole communion – the complete good.

"Was it apparition or merely the known reality of the hour past noon – in that lonely moment of ever – that I knew the flame; and whether in vaunted hubris, or in residual self-hate, I saw the flame, and wept, with moans and bending, that it was."

Elizabeth
"The Kept Ecclesia of Agatha Moi"

(of the emerald moth of the Limber lost)

Hinterlands:

Beginning Thoughts

Although the study of cognitive development began long ago, in more distant times, it was with the work of an Austrian physician, interested, himself, in a new advancement in medicine, proposed by Charcot in France, it involving the works\behavior of the mind (hypnosis) – it was these events, coming together that exploded the work of those with ponderings concerning behavior seemingly not fully understandable from known, casual factors. Sigmund Freud (1856-1939), he a neurologist, through clever observation and conversation came to explain the "mind" as a phenomenon divided into three portions of activity: the smallest, the knowing conscious; the second, larger, with stored material, but accessible with effort, and the largest, the unconscious, unknowing. This third position speculated that man was, most, unaware of his thoughts and feelings, and being more unaware, was therefore under the directives of the primitive unknown – not as reasonable as unreasonable.

Following closely, was a student who was interested in Freud's newly formed school of psychoanalysis, Carl G. Jung (1875-1961); Jung established the school of analytical psychology. As he studied and matured, he added, also, a fourth level of mental activity, the "*collective unconscious*," drawing from social and cultural influences, this level delving even further into the activity of unconscious thought, and its various manifestations.

These men influenced both Europe and the world tremendously, if having fallen away somewhat in today's thought. During the twentieth century, important areas of study saw their marriage of knowledge and insight: anthropology, literature, and medicine, generally.

It is from their announcement of the import of unconscious mental activity that vistas, varied and wide, have credited the thought not clearly known, but with effort and training, its then accessibility to allow the diversity of our world and lives to be realized.

Literature has produced record of many who have searched the self in unknown portions of the mind – that behind – the "hinterlands" – to find much beauty and truth. Swamps, bogs, marshes, the limber lost and the heath: all are greatly unknown in their darkness but possessing much beauty in presence and study. One's relationship with the grande natural and the arrangements within fraternity mirrors his inner self, and it, with God in Holy Presence.

Much of the Subjective ...

Much of the subjective in our thought is housed in what we call the "unconscious," – a principle, the history of its discovery already discussed, described first by Sigmund Freud, as early as the beginning twentieth century; his student, Carl G. Jung added to Freud's basic theory and their developing schools of thought grew to have a profound influence in Europe and the world. Basically, the thesis determined that we do not always" know" that that we do "know;" there can be activity of a cognitive nature in some level of consciousness unaware to our "conscious" mental activity.

When we speak of a subject, we most often give to it an objectively real presence, if it has qualities or properties which can be described. When we add other properties, those outside the "objectively real," we speak of metaphorical language, symbolism, and other particular terms. As abstraction becomes the more comfortably accurate avenue to the fuller meaning, we enter the psychological domain of characteristics and behavior. The meanings may take on dual characteristics, suggestions – those objective and subjective, resulting, at times, in powerful meanings and explanations that ordinary words or groups of words are unable to produce.

To rephrase the construct presented earlier, it is reasonable to suggest that we all, within ourselves, hold "hinterlands," swamps, bogs, marshes, limberlosts; and within these lie much of the insight and direction that prescribe our steps, whether followed throughout or no. We wander through the night and are troubled by "levels" of consciousness or cleverly clear unknowings such as that discussed in Ernest Becker's work, "*The Denial of Death*;" but the swamps, the brambles color the light in the eventual knowing. We delve, probe, seek, ponder and struggle; we meditate and pray, keeping always the truism of the priest-friend to the troubled, young instructor: "*We must presume good will.*"

Elizabeth
October 24, 2019

Cognitions

Cognitions are units of recognition which help us to organize our perceptive arena, manage our impulses and needs, and reflect on our motivations as they come to interact with circumstances produced by our environment. They are troublesome, often paradoxical, as well as healing, and contribute, at times, to problem solutions. Their basic (smaller) units are called "words," designed out the different cultures of which we are found to be a part.

These units suggest to us to reduce the large to that manageable, the small so that it is clear and observable, and that felt, but not understood, to become known, as the more simple and more meaningful. Called forth, then, are mechanics for understanding the good, the basic quality of beauty, the metamorphosing of all, and the intertwined existence of opposite feelings, the dispersion of dissonance to be nearly complete in the matter of truth.

Inside our thought holds most of the riddle of existence: we interact primarily with the objectively real, but always in companionship with the part of ourselves that is like an unclear halo. We know it is truly our own, but, in great part, clouded. It is the marvelous self that is non-corporal. It is the spiritual unit of our being, and while troubling and source to much sorrow, it is triumphant, as we die to its revealing, we, then, rising, as the grande phoenix out her ashes to the upward. It is truly a source of secrets, an entrance, however painful, for the Holy into our being; it allows a concept of beauty to blossom in heinous circumstance, and allows night to be born into a knowing glory, solitude, in onliness, to present honorable messages of truth.

Therefore, the bog, the marsh, the heath, in purple or grey – the bramble, yet the swamp – these are familiar settings for research and truth. Our cognitive skills and their enlightening studies in classrooms, everyday walks, traumatic events, as well as alternations in natural rhythming – these we bring inside ourselves to see what we may see – perhaps a rose; the rose grows into much of itself, into its rarity of beauty, within the dark, and as a metaphor of truth, more out of solitude and personal embracing of ultimately finding.

Elizabeth
October 22, 2019

Constructs in Unconscious Mental Activity

(our swamps, marshes, bogs and glens)

Review into recognition, association and chaining, transference and many other methods of managing our thoughts help in keeping and adding to our body of conscious knowledge. Reading the great works of literature is a profound good in acquiring information which can be helpful. A reviewed roll call, then, of some of our best minds, who in their works have said much – these bare excellent in example of building good cognitive skills and healthy thought.

We often say that history "began" when record was first kept. We have, indeed, a very long history of collected, and recorded cognitions. They speak as very wealth, heavy gold. Good vocabulary and style have been incorporated into the presentation of some of the best thought ever espoused.

Many of our earlier writers address their problem areas in poetry and prose, at times in music; most, however, have chosen the genre of narrative and lyric poetry. These are often impassioned conversations with their inner selves, inside their marshes, bogs, and swamps of thought, frequently, in part, unknown to them, except unconsciously. – depressive moods, pain, navigating with frightening steps –These entrances into the areas of thought "behind," – dark, uncertain, and often terrifying – these have left the thinker in earlier adventures despondent, fatigued unsure – and in a plethora of states, depending on the nature, the subject of the search, and its review.

In the pursuance of our lives, today, we are captivated by concepts such as "more," "different," "immediacy," and such so that having problems that involve "dark rooms behind" hardly have any place in our thought\existence at all. How small our horizons, the vistas, the wisdom we explore. It is a truism that pain often accompanies the exploring of these areas, but all who create beauty, the center of this true discussion, alongside happiness, peace and verity, find pain a most valued elixir to the phenomenon of creating. To create, in whatever area or degree of refinement is, yet, being for the moment, who we fully, truly are, contentedly – the accountability of us all, we, full, "lesser" gods.

Areas of our lives that hold more constant than not, offer the reservoir of thought that contains our certainties and uncertainties; these provide our joy, and our sorrow, producing the paradoxical nature of all humanity. These areas perform independently, and together, and it is a worthy moment spent examining them as they play out their qualities in our lives.

Night
Solitude
Nature
Beauty
Time
Space
Oneness

Hinterland Areas
of Knowing

Night

Other than being alone, night is our most familiar "hinterland;" it is truly "a room behind," the space allowed the unconscious, at various levels, to be ever present. It is dark, the antithesis of light and, unless altered, artificially, everywhere in its provided time. Thoughts erased by various forms of light, or necessary industries, concentration on other escapes – or meeting the specter that bides in thought – these, especially the latter, contribute to a resulting of psychic pain, if comprising some familiar, alternate avenues.

But there are positives that accompany the dark; calm, rest from various fatigues, and all such affords; reverie, recognition, even if painful, finding the self mirrored, in greater completeness: insight inside a spark of diversion – into peace. Thomas Becker wrestled with denial, a clever, necessary cognitive maneuver in the face of his impending death; he must to deal with the meaning of life: his valiant record, *"The Denial of Death,"* stating the reality we all must embrace, if we live effectively, was awarded the Pulitzer Prize two months following his death.

Solitude

As hinterlands be, solitude is a "state of being," yet not necessarily separate, wet, dark or isolated. An individual can be alone of others, or any *"dinga"* (Rilke's expression for "thing") in a variety of circumstances. Most think of solitude as a chosen period one wishes, or a time without the resources of camaraderie. It can be painful and frustrating, unproductive, most unhappy in lack of companionship. However, many seek this loneliness for various periods of time, for a variety of reasons. In solitude, one can be free of many realities with which he is not in love and charity; he can clear his thought of subjects that are negative, such as fear, regret, doubt, the entire arena of loss, allowing unconscious truths to press, but then such may be his whole wish. Prayer and dialogue with self (without reality's dress) and communing with nature can be purposefully pursued until answers, although emotionally fraying, can be found, allowing the weight of doubt to lessen toward a true respite.

Solitude, in a sense, allows conversation without courtesies – it permits the "raw" to emerge openly, so that examination and scrutiny can be effected concerning a problem area – a spade can be called a spade, and tolerated. One can achieve the realization of what objectively is without prescribed properties, placing realities where their true is observable. As Sidney Lanier, the early American, Southern poet insisted, he felt need to journey to the salt springs in Georgia to allow his conscious to journey still further, into his self to achieve spiritual union, especially to learn, through contemplation the value of patience and the all good, this experience recorded in his verse, *"The Marshes of Glynn."*

Nature

Charles Kinsley's statement *"Study nature as the countenance of God"* is, in truth, strong. Our early sages, thinkers, philosophers felt that nature was the only infallible constant we know, that it is the pattern we need to observe and study for the managing of our lives. Nature is difficult to fully understand, but its lessons teach us much, and simply so, about life and how to build and flourish.

Perhaps first to observe in nature is beauty - the seasons, the brush painting them across our days. It is constant in perishing and redeeming, all to the good. This lesson is one of the paramount subjects which lies, always, half asleep, half awake, in our unconscious self, our awareness of refuge and trouble.

Yet nature is a balm; it heals in example and experience. And if aging is one of the swamps\ bogs threatening us, nature shows how the different, the changing can increase, and remain in good; it can also affect as a great balm to soothe and heal loss, pouring out comfort and understanding as early American poet, Walt Whitman wrote following the death of President Lincoln in his verse, *"When Lilacs Last in the Dooryard Bloom'd:"* the star, (Venus), the bird's song (the brown Thrush), and the sweetness of the blooming lilacs – all forming a trinity of reminding, remembering, each year – senses, reason, understanding, together. Virgil was his model, inside the grande pastoral tradition, nature mourning the fall of a good man, with eulogy, procession, and other characteristics.

Readers of Father J. P. De Caussade are admonished to seek abandonment of self to Divine Providence. To the degree that such can be done, nature is the mirror to our steps, the world in its own, we in our own. The Priest Poet, G. Manley Hopkins, saw Holy Presence, most, best, in nature, its power and fury and its giving salvation – and he wrote masterfully of it. A more recent poet, twentieth century, American, James Whitehead wrote of human nature, its foibles, in the colloquial, quite the cavalier, but always concluded with the natural and true, intractable, hard, but true. In the final poem of his third book of verse, he speaks of his father:

> *"My father's a gentle Presbyterian*
> *At eighty, thoughtful, he believes in hell."*

The title of this above work is *Near at Hand*, taken from the words of Marcus Aurelius Antonius:

> *"Near at hand is the time when you will be forgetting all;*
> *Near, too, all forgetting you."*

Beauty

To discuss beauty as a hinterland approaches the awkward, the paradoxical, but our full understanding of its reality can find it better accomplished when we do. Our whole understanding of the concept   is thought of as only positive, and in reality, it is; it is just that it rests in the medium of complexity until we work through some of its particulars. In doing so, the result is althemore positive and lasting.

In beauty we find secrets – those that are confusing, hurtful, easily misunderstood; and so, the truth is that beauty is often painful, as in love. Miscommunication, body language, social requiring's and such can provoke loneliness, and regret, feelings of guilt, and doubt, loss, and sadness. Beauty in the unrecognized, the strange, and different; the sometime absurd, undervalued, or unannounced, yet bazaar – these are gifts only in instances of re-learning, casting off, and acquiring some amounts of newly discovered wisdom. Recognition and acceptance can then occur. Revealing, revelation can be happy experiences.

Lost beauty is among the most difficult arrangements of beauty which is to be worked into place with peace. The dark must be arranged behind, the hidden truths of the unconscious and unknowings, to rest aside through finesse and realization – these steps put in place facilitate the light of peace occurring.

True beauty resides in its verity. Working with our hinterlands and finding courage to pass through is growth that prevents disappointment and disillusionment – and ultimately fulfillment. Again, finding, reviewing, relieving, replacing and reassessing, enjoying true beauty can be accomplished in the full of abandonment. Alfred Lord Tennyson, one of the two giant British poets of the Victorian Period was a devout Christian until his best friend, in young adulthood, quickly succumbed to an aneurysm. Completely overcome by grief, and increasing doubt, twenty-six years passed before Tennyson "beat his music out."   The beauty of the friendship, which was finally established in proper setting, allowed grief to be placed in proper distance. The beauty of his peace at the twenty-sixth Christmas reveals his joy in passing through the hinterland of his friend's death:

In Memoriam, A. H. H.

I hold it true, whate're befall;
I feel it when I sorrow most.
'Tis better to have loved and lost,
than never to have loved at all.

Alfred Lord Tennyson

Time and Place

Time and place are not only Shakespearean "classic unities," observed in his drama, but they are classic unities in our everyday living. They provide the moment and setting for all our thought and behavior. These can be sequestered into a "room behind" for many reasons, often to the malnourishing of the soul. When we spend time too much to ourselves, we, being basically social animals, the matter of reciprocity is left wanting. Reciprocity indicates giving back, but actually it is part of an exchange; we learn to give and receive in the full act of reciprocating. Appreciation is a key factor in this lovely behavior.

Time away from the unacceptable business of light, distance, complacency, sloth – these interfere with fullness that can offer comfort rather than emptiness – ennui. Time filled with healthy engagements can allow for appreciation of wealth in hand, the glory of entering, emerging light and sentiments that accompany. Since space and time are fluid and wise, some of the ideas of Allen Watts might be referenced: Mr. Watts, a British thinker and writer during the sixties and seventies, was educated thoroughly in Zen, and, in this country, completed his divinity degrees. His wisdom shows in his publications, those celebrating the moment, the discharge of the concept of anxiety, and full understanding of the concept of God, since such is not humanly possible. His work, *The Wisdom of Insecurity*, is a passionate, if reasonable treatment of these ideas.

Space permits examination, a kind of weight station of all our goods; remembering can occur even if from hidden, painful resources, but to resolution. With wealth secured in hand we can enjoy, draw strength from "glories of the glories that have been." As the comforting reasonable gathers to us, and not with shock value, we, through organization, find hope and clarity in matters that require time, quiet, organization, review and accepting the seemingly impossible, so that special heights of thought and behavior are approachable.

We can know, then, the joy of entering emergency light, having prepared for dark, and finding courage to pass through to it.

(Much of the above material has reference to Dante's work,
"*The Divine Comedy, Part One The Inferno*.")

Oneness

Conclusions are more difficult than beginnings, simply because much has been opened and reviewed. Where, or when, then, do we feel that a completeness has been reached. We often do not, in even the briefest of exchanges. The human personality is rich and varied and worthy of much study.

If we research the unknowing of ourselves, and others, we find much that requires "saying," although there are those who choose the ascetic path, or some semblance of it, and are happy and productive with prayer, intra- psychic dialogue, and themselves, alone of others.

Love and companionship are the avenue most choose to fill their needs for another's soul to complement their own. Such is in motion, everywhere – lovely, passionate, casual, selfish, giving, broken, anti-troth and many variations on an old theme. For many, it is a rite of passage, a social game, or proof of certain qualities wished in one's own person. Happily, it is for some the grail which, when accomplished, will secure their bliss.

John Donne, an English cleric and poet, during the sixteen-seventeen hundreds, unhappily born -Catholic to become Anglican, endured throughout his life the unmet need of complete oneness. He wished a complete spiritual union with God through a mortal partner. He grieved the loss of the pastoral and the terrors of coming mechanization; he was married and was father to several but his work shows that he prayed with fervor and impassioned pleas for his wish that did not come:

> *"take me to you, imprison me,*
> *for I except You*
> *enthrall me,*
> *never shall be free,*
> *never ever chaste,*
> *except you ravish me."*

> *"The Holy Sonnets"*
> *Sonnet 14, "Batter My Heart"*

Houston Smith, scholar in religious studies in the United States, and one of the world's most influential figures in religious studies, was born in China to Methodist Missionaries. He remained Christian all his life, adding meditation to his devotional time. His works are very compelling, before his death in 2016 at age ninety-seven; in one of his most recent works, *"The Way Things Are;"* appears the quote below:

"The path, in part, in understanding 'the way things are' is in the wisdom garden of mine and others' hearts.

As beautiful as the sentiments are, in the lines quoted above, I felt, on first reading them, and of them, that I must rephrase them in the earliest years of taking up my pen, again, purposefully.

Two Poets

There are moments when my heart aches;
It sounds and radiates the colors of the sun and the rose.
I cannot know whether I feel great joy or heavy grief,
only that I feel that there is a wanting need
to tell another.
Andso, I will show to you the furnishings of my heart,
and you of yours to me.
And we will stand, together,
two poets,
with a quiet annunciation.

The provided yearning of the human heart which promotes, for a beautiful interlude or
a grande eon – a portion of oneness – is most complete in that
part – not ever to be lost – for the heart does not forget.

"– Celestial airs,
thy breathing comes to me,
of life in one of two –"

"la Libellule"
Elizabeth

It may be that the final verse in the "Oneness" discussion could fashion a workable plan for
successful togetherness; it was an early poem, read by my nephew, Jason, who commented: "I
want to memorize it, so that it will always be with me," – the first of my verse committed to
memory, and its sentiment holding fast!

Elizabeth
January 24, 2020

Contents

Preface\Introduction

It may be that the "hinterlands" giving most bounty to our queryings lie in our cognitive holdings. While visions, dreams, apparitions, as well as recalled fable and myth construct much of our milieu of existence, they involve impulses emitting from the "old brain," instinctual responses, the energy of the driving passion of Eros toward survival and procreation. Our cognitions, following the evolved advent of recognition, object labeling, words and ideas, beginning associations, transference and such – these do embrace all that said earlier; nonetheless, the full process may be described as cerebral activity comprising the grandly active larger pulse that reverberates as the knowing of ourselves and our world, it being accomplished – if yet, founded, in the womb of darkness – factors we may not ever understand or explain.

In conception, we begin first growth into life, in complete ease, with every need satisfied, this circumstance forming a bond which at birth becomes a longing for oneness that is most often not met, after birth. We bring forth, out circumstance, more circumstance, and search their corners all of our lives.

Within this need begins the progressive construct of freedom, as a possible solution, but it is encased, so, in still, endless need. (W. Wordsworth, John Donne) Freedom is a principle which drives to destruction, merely the "death" in life while in the womb – the security without boundaries, except that boundaries are, and they restrict as we grow, in all areas, finally to expulsion, to begin again, not in dark unknowing, but into lighted knowing, and unknowing, ultimately into again, eternal night. The only form of true freedom is in innocence, from truth that is taught by example, authority being of reason, acted out in daily living.

These circumstances, evolving with experience, instruction, observation, and the residual pattern of factors in exiting the womb, remain in part, unclear; they exist in evolving levels of consciousness of which we stand unaware, afraid, partially knowing, perhaps always seeking – finding as our steps of dust allow.

The diminutive, and, it in shadow, offers most suggestions to understanding questions of almost any subject, and it is in the "hinterlands" of self that we find a wealth of knowing by adding consciously to the suggested "bleeding through."

Many variables contribute to the self, understandings of ideas and our existence in its full will, fears, unexplained motivations, and abilities, with very myriads of other factors making their appearance in the "small" miracle of conception. The following is the available history of the world we know, and that which sleeps under its grande, unknown influence.

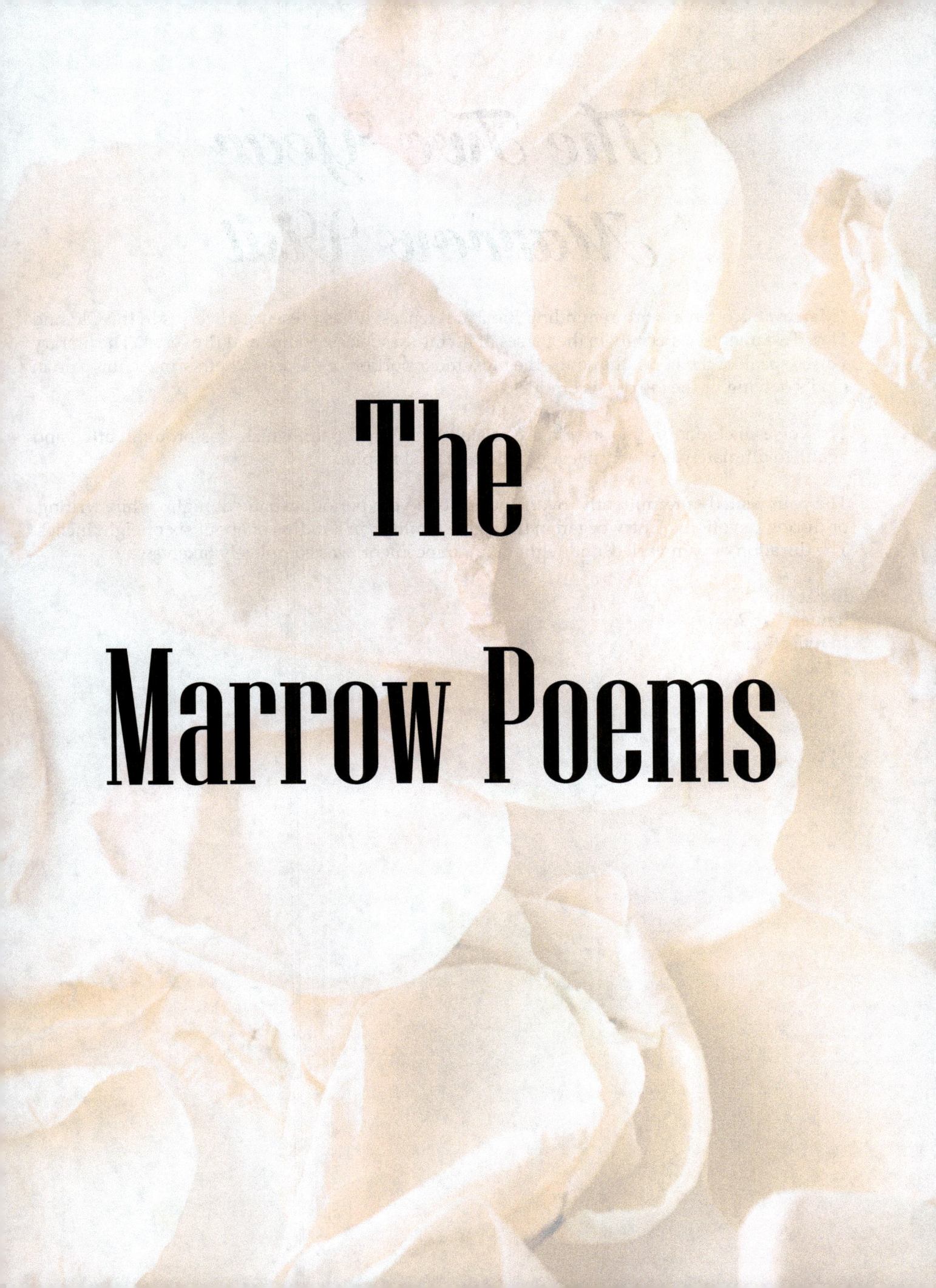

The
Marrow Poems

The Two-Year Marrow Visit

"Marrow" is often a word reminding Biblical refences; it has presence in verses in the Old and New Testaments, especially in the verses of literature such as Psalms and Proverbs. The literary verses speak of the heart, the soul – the most inner portion of the self, whether in feeling pain in God's delving or the joy of His kindness.

The verses included in this section are related to physical pain, which was brought, often and again, to ultimately bathe in sweet peace and a final respite.

The pain visited, intermittently, over a nearly two-year period, usually at night, while writing, or during devotions. Entry began in the right shoulder, in a radius of about six or eight inches. The duration of pain varied, and without announcement, was completely taken away.

Elizabeth
January 20, 2020
In reflection

Oh Holy, and Able Presence...

O Holy, and Goodly Able Presence,
Thou Who enters into the marrow,
Extending my peace throughout that of the reaching,
And touching arm –
Thou Who art able to, yet, caress dreams
So that they find, again,
Passion and will to continue –
Thou – come close, more, to me
For despite terrestrial bindings,
My earthen complexions –
My helpless needs –
It is so of willingness
That I love Thee.

Elizabeth
On passing into sleep, remembering an image
Of several nights past –
June 12, 2017
Near eleven o'clock pm

Oh My Soul

Oh my soul, my marrow is nearly stolen
Away by the watchful hours of waiting.
The day came, putting away the night,
And it bore well the becoming good day it was.
Beauty and hope in necessary steps,
Good fatigue in looking behind,
With these the sun came into its closing glory,
And all was counted, and lost to twilight.
But my heart knows more the dark than the light:
Come, come, with candle and lamp;
Let there be voice in echoing thought,
And a perceived touch in moving shadows.
Thou had'st come into my jointed marrow,
And, as Thy porcelain doll,
Wrapped me in care and softest instruction.
Bruise me with your tenderness,
And free me from my emptiness,
Filling the hurt of absent peace
With Thy wholeness.

Elizabeth
July 7, 2017
At twilight, at Elizabeth House, alone

Held Up the Day

The flower of night spreads full
Across the dark, and dreams embroider
Golden stamen with silver pistols,
The breathing of shadowed rest
Gently nourishing.
There is no sound or press,
No diligence to discharge,
Only the peace of restful beauty
To be tasted midst darkened nectar
That smooths the day
Into the placid night.
Resurrection nearby, the laying on of hands,
The incense of passing spirits:
Thou had'st held me up the day,
And night promises the passing of all fatigue.
Like starlight, drifting downward,
Peace touches gently,
And once again my marrow,
Wounded in requiring steps,
Becomes tenderly ministered unto,
Into peace and earthly repose.

Elizabeth
2017

Thee, Thee

Thee, Thee, Thee and me,
Thou in my heart, alone, Thee filling
In my complete barren,
My darkness without light.
I feel Thee in my marrow, Thy port of coming in,
Through pain, into peace,
And safety of the shepherd's fold.
Give me, Thee, strength to reason, to press,
To wait on Thy always abundant mercies;
Let me be strong enough to sound,
An instrument of Thy love,
That it reflect back to my own,
That I know joy and peace in full
Contentment.

Elizabeth
11/25/2017
Thursday night, ten-thirty pm

Lord have mercy;
Lord have mercy;
Lord have mercy.

Small, constant prayer of Russian Orthodox friends

Entering Again

Thou had'st entered my own again,
But not in jointed pain,
But in an effervescing fragrance
Of Lilly and first falling starlight.
Thou had'st come to secure, and hold,
To comfort and balm,
These joyful touches bringing a peace that burkes
All strife and lays out, as a sweet fair linen,
The grace of a giving Master to his own.
How much do I weep, how long do I pray,
How often do I bow –
Enough to, in my full willingness,
Love Thee –
And to find fellowship
With Thee.

Elizabeth
August 10, 2017, near midnight
After dark, a coming, fresh imbuing of Thy Presence:
Comfort, understanding, confidence and peace – the ease of Thy Porcelain doll –

... I Ask

In all humility, I ask –
In the night's truest deep –
Strength for coming steps,
And certitude of Presence in all,
That of the warmth of a knowing isness,
The oneness of true salvation.
To be wrapped as in fair linen,
And open to receive the full weight
Of most forgiveness,
And coming good –
Let, in this resplendent pasture,
This unending, and giving, fold –
In these grande strength of Thy holiness,
The unapproachable fullness of Thy Being;
The omniscience I cannot even humbly comprehend,
Let the little stings, yet, the fiercest dragons
Which punctuate familiar and necessary,
Still, farthings, and furlongs.
Let these find no refuge from Thy eye,
No saving from Thy hand.
And I grasp my respite,
To feel the eternal truth,
Of my burden upon
Thy generous bosom.

Elizabeth
December 17, 2016
Near twelve-thirty am

Come, Come to Me

Come, come to me: come to me,
While my thought is reaching,
My heart, open to accepting;
While in the folding of hands, come,
The joint's marrow aching of Thy need;
While bowing in deference, do come, come to me.
Know to me the steps of wisdom,
And grant to me in moments, still,
With lovely images inside –
Come, come to me.
Behold, an effervescent beauty, a shining ladder,
The sweet moisture of waiting faith –
Ascending, and descending, up to Thee,
And down to me.
Thou had'st come, in my love's most need, to me.

Elizabeth
October 1, 2017

Oh Thee

Oh Thee, the night is in its deep,
And my marrow knows
The pain of the unknown,
Of flesh that cannot but be consumed.
Come Presence, and as the joint did once receive,
Let Thy onliness of grace know my need.
My strength is, now, like the green blade,
Reaching upward to its Lord;
Grant more and more the hope
That rests in my willingness to love Thee,
That I find Samaritan balming in the portion
Which only Thou can give.

Elizabeth
In deepest night
July 5, 2017

Come...

Come, now, into my beggar soul,
Into my marrow,
Infuse, into, Thy strength;
Forget in me the forward steps that the days,
Yet the seasons hold out towardward.
Soften the pain of loss,
And store in keeping fears
That supplant the marrow's faith;
Let, please, yes, please
Thy goodness
Traverse the way
Of greater peace.

Elizabeth
June 16, 2017
Eight o'clock am

Thought Marrow

HolyFatherGod,
Thou had'st entered my marrow once more,
Only, now, not in the joint of the arm,
But in the bend of thought.
The pain is heavy, but as gentle as reason can give:
Lost kin, lost friends, time passed,
And sentiment, spent.
I know, still, that the emptiness left is more
The room of thy mercies;
Give me, then, full accepting, full reaching spirit
For the more comfort of this harbor
In Thy bosom.
Amen.

Elizabeth
November 25, 2017

The Catching Red Bloom

Bless mon Coeur;
Yes, be He who clasps the hand
Of his infant own.
The day is worn and spirits fatigued;
Still all appears, yet, as a lengthy journey
Entering its short denouement.
Take the willing, small hand that extends
From within the center marrow
Of the red rose bloom,
And let the bloom catch the divinity
Of immortal love,
Safety and peace.

Elizabeth
January 29, 2020
-long day, drifting downward-

Reference to John Donne

Throughout my work, I frequently reference John Donne, the sixteenth-seventeenth century English, cleric poet who spent the whole of his emotional striving searching for a oneness with God through a mortal relationship. His intense fervor in this matter is perhaps most beautifully written into his work, *"The Holy Sonnets," "Batter my Heart,"* particularly – pieces I do often reference.

Elizabeth
January 26, 2020

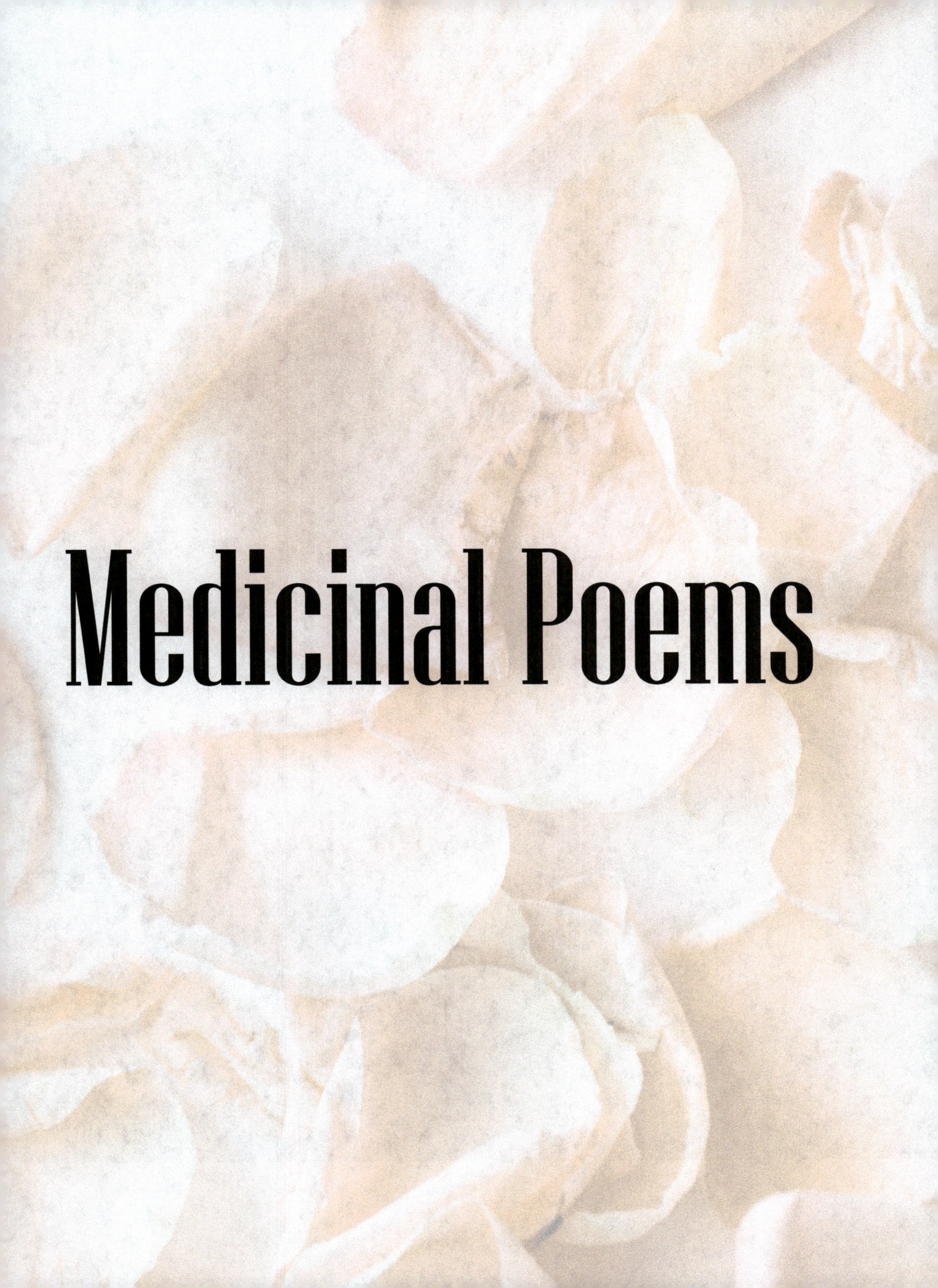

Medicinal Poems

Solace

Medicinal Poems' Accompanying Remarks

The eight verses following, evolved out desperate attempts at finding some so-
lace in a difficult circumstance. The night was the first of true cold in the new
season; it was a night of lunar fullness, and all of the earth knew so.
I had, for reason of incompetence, no anti-anxiety medication for four days and
nights, and was experiencing withdrawal in the added anxiety of its absence.
Three severe anxiety attacks occurred in little more than an hour, with-
out any available emergency help, leaving me exhausted in the addition-
al state of lack of sleep in the days and nights without proper medication.
The mind always protects itself, when the world, and its others, do not un-
derstand, and become unkind; we try, then, to find a safe place.
I composed, transcribed and recorded these little pieces in a matter of several scattered hours.

Elizabeth
November, 2019
In deepest night

Strength Between

Within the faith of all Abrahams,
Inside the security from
Combined furlongs
Of the Arc;
About, the imaged beauty
Of brown bird
Touching lilac sweetness –
Between the golden weight of these,
Lies measure of the strength of Majesty,
Grace and love.

Elizabeth

Seasonal Hour

Red-striped, white carnations,
Spread small and wide,
Behind, yellow and copper-rust of others –
Speak now, these,
The day of lost summer,
The bringing in of dark, and close;
Moments of thought,
Reverie, warmth and good.

Elizabeth
November 1, 2019
Dusk\twilight
-a very difficult night, and day, following –

Dew-light Grace

Come, come dew-light of sweet olive mist;
Kiss with your fragrant touch
My eyes, my cheeks, my lips,
So that I know the favor of thy freshness,
All about my senses,
In this althewhile of pain and sorrow.
Come into my heart,
My beggar soul,
Your grace and love
Of terrible majesty.

Elizabeth
November 1, 2019
Ten o'clock, evening

Eves

Solemn eves, joyful in their bittersweet;
To come and be, to in their coming,
Living the reality of their dream –
To hold until – to bring again,
To clasp into image
And conscious arranging:
How to, how does their isness live
Into the morrow;
Time, imaged past,
Is time in the moment,
Observed, and all of Tense
Is merely thoughtfulness.

Elizabeth
November 1, 2019
Early dark

Now

Now is difficult,
Now is being in the alone;
Now is as forgotten,
Mirrored an unfamiliar shadow.
Powered by idea, ignited by senses,
Now is a passage to another hour,
An hour of the reality of the singular_
Awake in a sleep,
A dream that is cruel
In its conscious knowing.

Elizabeth
November 1, 2019

Comely Gift

In the night, and in the day,
Thou does't command,
I, to comply;
For in Thy pleasure lies infinite peace,
And strength of history's legions, gold.
Let me come, let me be,
In comfort's quiet and lovely ease –
The dark as comely, as soft like giving touch,
Surely, in its true,
Its divine gift.

Elizabeth
November 2, 2019
In deepest night
On fifty-five, early morning

Hearth Echoes

When we are alone,
And dark is full about,
Lamps remain with their constant glow,
But we continue by separate moments, only –
The long way home.
White clouds are, still, perhaps, in memory,
With mornings at a fanciful distance;
Presently, quiet softens the hours,
The silent voices, within,
And content becomes a treasure
As childhood, passed,
It captured over and again,
As the mystery of Christmastime,
Joyous,
Echoed all around the hearth.

Elizabeth
Early November, 2019

The Hallucinatory

Poems

Brief summary of "The Hallucinations"

The time, over which I have just passed, reminds a "long ago" with dark and difficulty beyond ordinary description. It was "hard" winter, heavy and without convenient warmth, lacking sunshine, yet that smooth and sterile steel, smiles of various light, but with promise, only they not to become.

This winter was not there, and then it waited in every corner, crouching, departing and stalking the hours between and within my rooms, throughout thought and waiting consciousness – and doubts at every wind's blow, the slightest perpendicular becoming a figure to be done with cognitive battle.

Doubts hissed like frightened geese chilling, piercing together with the wind, the darkening inside a heaviness – a day making steps of staggering effort at standing with confidence.

My thoughts bled out strange mirrors of the world I stood within: no sound out silent stares but dark voice and unkindly form ever present. Vestiges of sacred thought and long waking of future encounters persisted.

Laughter, at times, was suggested within frenetic activity – decorating, dancing, fondling my paintings, re-dressing their frames, all to return to their "normal" selves when the frenzy settled into the old sameness.

The extreme activity, laughter, frightening activities, especially when music would sound, pushed me to exhaustion, to hold my plume and record or else run in panic downstairs where the figures rarely came.

My thought almost losing consciousness, or more losing comfortable composure, I suffered the question of why and what, yet where to – this macabre masque that seemed to portend my end. In deepest fear imaginable – where would I eternally bide.

I then became awake, always, not to move, to effect any change that would add confusion or any of the adverse. Surprisingly, the figures could appear gentle, especially within my screams and sometimes when my violent exchanges occurred. So strange – the tryst with these together: so much confusion to begin, and, nothingness, other than in conclusion.

Silence within excited activity, dangerous symbols and movements as in the burning cross being rushed toward me; fixed staring, out bodies black and brown without features, or with oversized body parts, and few of the masculine gender. Both genders were represented in the leading hierarchy, however. It was not unusual, these alone, sometimes feigning life creatures moving about toward me after often purposeful, magical mannerisms that seemed, perhaps, as play. And punishment waited with the obscure and the fear of the full manifestation of the supposed forward steps.

And then something – a call, a plea, he, it, with water – nothing, a half something – all the while the all continued, into finality – visitors not alive, chemistry, active, alive following continuously into lines and contours of fuller completion.

There is no antidote to truth, save that in its all fullness.

Elizabeth
June 19, 2018
Just at bedtime

The Preview

Like angelic innocence rebuffed,
Turned aside, the night would not wrap its rest around me;
Fatigued in steps, thoughts losing awareness –
All before pressed to come, again:
Startled awakening into open consciousness
That was not friendly;
More, it leaned into threatening in a strange,
Bizarre new reality.
Up then, down the stairs, opening the door to all outside;
And running, running, down the drive,
Rocks cutting my bare feet, but to safety.
How now – again, the ambiance, again?
Of quickness, wakefulness, a heavy coverlet
Of stimulation out a body of finished day:
The mania will bring delight,
And fancies I cannot understand –
Colorful confusion into fear –
The ecstatic, in its strangeness, absurdity,
With its dark flowers,
Falling into a maelstrom that whirls in grey and black,
Pulling downward, into a cursed nothingness.
-to sleep, please, on rosen petals, inside the warmth of light,
And within a peace of a chosen emptiness –

-until next time – the foreboding – sudden, unableness
To find sleep, fearing the coming of dark images –
Apparitions, without their dress of white –

How do we,
In what fashion of deliverance –
Do we live together as human animals –
When we are instructed in every medium
To live as gods.

Elizabeth
First of many nights of the beasts
Troubling thought
April, 2018

And when clouds begin to gather light behind,
And imaginings out fatigue and rest call within,
Spreaded wide becomes my soul with heart
All inside my handsome, feathered plume,
It made splendid, sparkling new by
Dew of first evenfall –
With contours fair, sunset hues of melloned Rose
And starlight, with flowing rouge,
A portrait of love and gratitude has come,
Passionate and true.
Ah, Baal, with streaming color of heavy gold,
Strong, intractable –
Stand ever still with metallic heart, in awe and helplessness,
Motionless in full unknowing help,
To melt into a pool of golden blood,
Streaming warm, and full, with loss and unkind knowing.

On trying to remember a lost verse: the exercise
March 18, 2017
Before the full period of "beasts"

Slay Me Not

Slay me not, today
But rather let Thy breath fall over me
That I continue moist and temperate with life.
Let the sun fall on me, for I have need of light,
The generous reminder of Thy golden benevolence.
Slay me not, today, of my own arrows,
But allow all faith and trust
To hold up my tenuous soul.
Let not foreign dreams,
Though within my night of Thee,
Gather about in daylight hours,
But be held in capture
Until I find my fending strength, again.
Slay me not this day, for I am not counted among
Heathen raging nor hypocritical voicings,
But stand with humble gratitude
To find merciful God
Who sees the expanse of all souls.
Slay me not this day,
But let early Roses bunch and show
Their only rouge to cold sunlight,
For they speak well of Thy terrible majesty,
One of Thy holdings of the many
Voices of Truth.

Elizabeth
February 10, 2019

Coming Dark

In these final hours of day,
In challenging, full press of tense
Of which we still know,
But without the majestic eye –
HolyFatherGod, could that always there be light –
Grace here, grace there, ever then as now grace,
For steps that come in the night may be of gravest
Revelation and realities,
Steps fearful and requiring.
Soften, then, the stillness, enter dark
On the arms of stars, letting it wander,
As a wind, a cloud, aside,
In the smile of her grace, the moon.
Pour faith into a thousand vials,
Legion lights, small into flowing,
And this into a silence;
Let the eyes of those whose cups of mystic nectar
Have fallen on their side –
Let these, and all souls, find dark
A truly sweet unknown.

Elizabeth
April 29, 2018
At midnight

-the possible visit of images, tonight-
-the wind and cloud metaphor from conversation with Joseph this evening;
I have great loss in saying goodbye to the day-

All Night

As stones forming a corner,
Through long, dark hours,
I *"beat my music out."*
And finally, in the mercy of exhaustion,
Birds began to sing the Magnificat that birds sing;
Dogs wakened to bark in spirited no-tones,
And insects sound in different unisons
The background of today's melody:
-the bells-
They become recognizable in the morning's silence,
Symbolizing my own person in the nothingness they bring.
Their images evolve into that becoming truths,
Remaining with their hidden messages,
To discover presently.

Life is so much struggle, especially so
When it is always turning out of sight;
But the beauty of the struggle is the finish
Of the jewel.

Will and insight are balanced in most instances,
But will can be usurped by some
Combinations of circumstance;
We find we are subject to that we cannot
Understand or truly accept. We fight,
We struggle in dissonance, or we withdraw
Into a kind of falling; our menu is determined by a myriad
Of factors, those arising out of flesh and spirit.

_Out the menagerie of morning sounds which did not come fully –

Elizabeth
April 29-30, 2018
All night, in my chair
"We are prisoners in a halo of light."

Stay by Me

Stay by me, still,
Hold to me, close;
Breathe gently
Thy strength into me,
And arrange, around,
Pomegranates so that variegation
Of rose will, with soft passion,
Gentle my seeing.
I am alone except that Thou
Hold'st close all
Thy Porcelain dolls,
That they be safe,
And learn a coming content.

Elizabeth
April 12, 2017
In deepest night

Just at Bedtime

For all the warm smooth of giving dark,
Its smile that falls a blessed cosem;
Its tenderness in the softening of particulars
That daylight moments call to continuously be addressed;
For a peaceful silence, wide and covering,
Which pronounces a finishing,
A benediction to the day –
Mighty God, receive our thanksgivings;
Let us ledger, in passing into sleep,
The blessings of the filled day,
And, more, oh God,
The blessed promise of tomorrow,
Garnishing the whole of ourselves
With effervescing pearls,
Falling, all about us,
A well spring of ever –
All, that we sleep in hope
And trust, into Thy unknowing,
Yet Thy magnanimous grace,
Together with blessings
Unto keeping in all our need.

Elizabeth
July 30, 2019
Eleven o'clock pm
Just at bedtime

Silence in a beast undrawn quite beyond
Design and weight,
Having no master –
Like biting into stones lifted out the inferno:
No movement, no sound
But wasting strength within fiercest flame.
Crushing can come in time,
But blooms the dark blossom of the taste of harsh texture
And poor vaporous energy of odious nature.
And when the stones are crushed,
The silence broken, there is,
Most, the faintness the pallored pale
Of spirit given over to heaviest task.
The joy of sound fragrances lifting,
Colors pouring out layered melodies are

Unknowingly pressed closer by the truth in kept chambers
Of the spectre of energy;
It waits in the shadow,
That of endless store of dark solitude,
To be well to some spirits,
But of the whole that is,
Strikes in place as the true sword of emptiness,
Of the great house of nothing,
Of naught to reach to perceive,
The truest pain of insignificance
In the eternis.

Elizabeth

And so we joust to convince
That we win in peace,
To, with pain
Never to be drawn,
Know that we are each,
Only each,
With companion merely
Inside or to the fore
Of our shadow.

Elizabeth
September 2, 2006
Alone, somehow trying to communicate
With the emptiness, but futile.

A Wandering Dream

Coming beautiful,
Many days we wander
Through our dream;
The story of a garden and its steps
To an inclusive nailing –
We wander, more,
Bitterly, lovely,
Through our dream.
And conditional love grew forth the wager,
It difficult, yet with all good;
Still, many days,
These left to wander
Through our dream.
And long, constructing a more close theorem,
That of composites,
Left, nothing – no peace, then afforded in acceptance –
Ah, beautiful, many days come,
Always, to wander –
Always –
Left to wander in bitter sweetness,
Through our dream.

The arrangement is admirable,
And full of fairest glory,
The taking, bittersweet,
The vinegar and the thorns.

Elizabeth
(undated)
The time of the images, the hallucinatory "beasts"
April 30 – early May, 2019

Ill- fated Three

An *Usher* wind, surly,
With darkness of a maelstrom
Too intense to be adequately described,
Yet, for skillful metaphorical saying –
Such are my fears in the night –
The background against which I stand
Bares color and sound,
With the artist's intensity,
Suggesting threatening hoards mounted
On their beasts,
The very epitome of most formidable strength.
But for me, inside my own,
I know no advocate, to rise and stay the force
Which appears to ready a strike.
All is within thought, a bramble of lost safety,
Boundaries and strategies, rethought,
And removed – I to wander,
Ill-fatedly into, about –
Unknowing, beside truth – and these unacknowledged –
They bludgeon my failing strength of spirit;
And the ability, the lost will to separate,
To label, and act – these leave me more alone
As I reach toward images only imagined –
In the covering emptiness.
-Ah, *Ilyich*, I fear, I most fear – thy conclusion
Before your appointment with the poor bed,
It, in its shadowed reality, in the distant, unscheduled train,
The station which sponsored no known destination.

Elizabeth
December 18, 2016
Early morning\deepest night

-the bed and train station can be referenced to the true death of Leo Tolstoy;
Tolstoy was a devout Christian (Orthodox), almost an acetic in his later years;
But he wrestled valiantly with the fear of death, all of his life.
His work, "*The Death of Ivan Ilyich,*" is recognized as one of the world's
Masterpieces regarding the subject of death. Tolstoy died at a great age, alone,
In a deserted, isolated train station, on a poor, unkept cot –

Note of reference regarding *Ill-fated Three*

The omniscient observer\narrator, the "third" of the "ill-fated three," is I, Elizabeth, speaking in gentle understanding of two characters who are major players in the very fine works of two early modern authors: Usher, of "*The Fall of the House of Usher*," by American poet and short story writer, Edgar Allen Poe; and Ivan Ilyich of the treatise on death, "*The Death of Ivan Ilyich*," by Russian author of narrative, Leo Tolstoy.

All are ill-fated through the flaw of unhealthy needs of self.

Again, to Sleep

The days gracefully wander into golden,
Giving grandeur of promised life:
Our steps renew and enter, again,
The challenge of being.
The familiar, the novel, they have the light
Together; and in silence, within,
We embrace, and in more silence, within,
Of the maelstrom of fuller understanding,
We grieve.
Outside the glass, the chime hangs motionless,
The dark stillness an unheard "Amen"
To the accepted reality.

I can sleep, again, when coming daylight reigns,
It, the full keeper of all good.

Elizabeth
October 10, 2017
Early waking, near five o'clock am

A Yearning

A yearning which is unclear, but with prophetic suggestions,
Is with its press, familiar in its left fatigue.
And curiously, throughout, it is quite lacking in passion,
The salt without its savor.
In present moments, true, pouring awareness over my thought,
My whole sentiment finds a wish for a grand shadowing,
A somberness of ancient shade filled nearly completely
With the moment – wet with life and fullest understanding,
Purist, stately white, courting malady with reasoning.
The briefly passing light, through present, hanging grey
Leaves, hold tender strains of yesterday,
And furtive glances into tomorrow, but without treasured,
Sweet pain of former times.
More to my heart, I wish – somehow, in some fashion –
To know the complete of particular, small stings;
The rushing thunder of certain malignant movements;
The reality of the fable of beauty, and the crashing omega
Of the Alpha in eternity's given power.
For in my belly is an emptiness of peace, and in waiting,
Beside, perhaps above beauty and ease;
It arranges in thought before presenting to sentiment;
This peace shows the metamorphosed of all,
The final turn, the circle completing.
And if this shadowing falters my will, then I wish to begin again
With the strength I catch from the baton my former self passes –
To press again, with new, first passion –
For the gift of awareness is couched in the dew on able lips –
Ah – the adventure into which I am now growing is Kafkaesque,
Full to satiation: must then accept offer of future steps –
Celestial dust, far into the shadows of new awakenings.

Elizabeth
2018

Through the Night

Laws and theorem help keep us free,
But unsuccessfully.
Our words are pitiable – over and over again,
The same; the allowance for error leaves
No allowance for freedom –
And so we choose ought in sea of torture between.
But where left is the sea of doubt:
It remains – everywhere.

Darkness of night is a sea – that of sounding
Wooden timbers and the songs of the natural;
They give pause, repeatedly, to reflection
And expectancy, specters of the un-knowing, into knowing.
Shackles of a man in a sea of psychic pain between light,
And poorly seeing –
And there is the space of doubt,
Without tenets said, or intuition –
Of isolation and humility.

Our bellies tell us of the strength of our faith,
Its dark beside its light.
We waver on the Janus wisdom of faith –
In much, secure, while biding, always,
The fever of doubt.

Always, always working toward resolution –
We at times arrive, but over, and again, falter.
We arrive, spent in death,
In reality or metaphorically.

Elizabeth
April 29-30, 2018
Through the night –

Living is, most, a sometimes comfortable
Tryst with the familiar, punctuated by the novel and,
Oftentimes, aberrantly convincing.

In gracious, first moments, the sun is in all brightness
So that I cannot look fully into its gold;
Yet, darkness and loss have found the shade
Of my frame, and I hold close to myself this containment,

For I know of shadow and its clever attendants,
I, attempting a flourishing in their absence.
To flourish, I must look about, and up,
To let my ideas ride the sun's liquid countenance
Into the world of abstractions –
Entering and departing as drifting fragrances –
These to the needy self,
Of expectancy and will, beside.
Bide with me, bide with me words and songs,
Bells, contours lovely, and steps and streams of color,
Helping toward giving peace;
Let flowers strew their essence
Into my own, that I know the message of my hands,
My thought and seeing –
Of images that chorus forth the sunlight of all good.

Elizabeth
January 3, 2018
Noon into mid-afternoon
Breaking Ativan

The eternal God is thy refuge, and underneath are the everlasting arms.
There is an intermittent coming in the afternoon,
Before the still of night,
A great widening, more, an evenness
Which smiles into a kind of fantasia of contentment,
One without many necessary questions
Or backward glances.
All about is somehow "*as close to as it should be,*"
Or perhaps the issuing out of the energy left of spending.
Memory becomes more a gentle exercise
Then piercing sentiment, and tomorrow leans into
A kind of fancy which anymore bows less and less to responsibility;
And the old truths remain and are turned over and over again,
More comfortably, in song and narrative.
Goodbyes are sometimes hurried, sudden,
But often long and long,
For the reality of acceptance is difficult,
Wounding passively with a pain not easily recognizable
Or given to description, but catching,
In time, its own eventuality.

The days give ever generously, to take back again as well;
And in our knowing, great the lost, unhappily,
Great the distance of our closeness –
As much so as the reality of the failing,
Come gathered togetherness.

Elizabeth
August 14-16. 2017

The isolation of moving away from our first, and middle fullness,
To the fiercely holding to individual selfhood: the sad fortune of the *"fittest"* –

Thoughts in early morning; solemn thoughts just at bedtime –
Solemn but somehow as per my themes scripted, not so disquieting

Strange Climes

I find myself in strange climes, presently;
I have few boundaries outside those I impose,
Andso, there is little in containment.
This circumstance frees me of prescribed dissonance,
Or anticipatory angst,
But I feel pressed that I am not defined enough
To celebrate a self.
Surely, freedom is energizing, but mine is a forced choice,
And, therefore, I feel bowed low –
No expectation, without forward castings,
Eventually, still –
Checkmate.

Elizabeth
-thoughts while resting on a very "unrequiring" Saturday morning –
April 26, 2014

I have worked very intensely to become independent, and free of restric-
tions; how foolish to think of "being free" as being liberated from all –
Extremes have never been successful –
Again, I am, victoriously, lost.

Sheep and goats are truly different – not all herded animals, alone;
Fragrant Gardenias, with deep red garnet stones,
Coming with weepings, and obscenities – did come, did come –

Dreamtruths

Dreamtruth, dreamtruth, your coy, cognitive
Maneuvers elude me, quite with a master's skill.
Small, suggesting reminders invite
At first consciousness, in yet a darkened nature
So that I become fatigued with your clever finessing.
But not an angry heart provides your movements,
Your spritely entries and departures,
For your true devotion rests in my safety of reason.
I salute you, while admonishing some further
Revelation, for, still, I fear
Consequences of my own thought within the day.
Give to me, generously, images with clarity,
Full beauty on appearing,
Full knowing at departing.
If movement could hold color,
Let the stage be lighted, that an ambiance
Of joyfulness hang about my recognitions, and understandings.
Oh wisdom, court my awareness with adolescent
Anticipation to which fear is not an intruder.

Elizabeth
June 13, 2014
Having wakened from deep sleep, and knowing that I
Had dreamed about many "things," some leaving a shadow,
But I could not bring them, again, fully to the fore –

Variations on Night-time

Night-time quiet is gracious, a lady of noble estate,
Making all about – gentle, soft,
And without any governing inequality.
Only shadows indicate life,
And for the close of chariot wheels spinning, voices,
Uncontrolled, and violent movements that can sponsor in light –
Such of night is good, such of night is –
In its dew, good.
Yet, so – turning the leaf to its other side –
In reflection, and pensive mood, embracing widened
Thought occurs in moments such, destroying colored activity,
As if it be present, now, to this clay,
The recognizable all, east of time true.
Thought out this conscious graciousness –
Dark, then – and so, yet –
Or, in all otherwise – arrangements:
"How many times will I die."
Dying is a lonely confrontation with time –
For it is individual, and crosses, vestments, and pleading oblations –
These can only soften.
As appointments – and appointments – neither do they always ease –
For we die through variations of hurt and loss,
Yet reflection, through time passing,
Through beauty fading – just as surely as the ritual –
The hourly struggle, that of catching,
Holding; expressing in respite;
That lost to live, to leave all to those who cannot know good –
The final glorious, the truest equalizer –
The triumphant, closing breath.

Night, oh night, when mischief can ride with the highwayman and the kingly –
Ease out, lie quickly, into knowing – blessed night –
Be thy other visage, and fold close the heart that is kindled with peace.

Elizabeth
In deepest night, with burking the ungood –

-very ill, with heavy medication, thoughts, a burdensome bramble
December 1, 2014

With the absolute glory of the glories we have seen,
We become fatigued with questioning,
The doubting\dissonance, and struggling to live
As we have before; we wish for answers, but inevitably fall back to only
That which we have already known.
Such is not weak, aberrant, evil
Or any of such worded complexion.
We fight as we live:
With the resources we have;
Their origin, their strength and igniting are not
So important as their full possession,
This matter, altogether, yet, shadowed.

Elizabeth
December 16, 2017

And we may, then, play as dancing gazelles at Christmastime,
To full breathlessness, happy to slumber under the adolescent's softly falling stardust.
Ideas enter gently into the unstructured unconscious,
Leaving formalized truths,
Those sometimes long arriving in their maturity.
Such is sweet, and such is sad,
But a constancy much as the present cadence of December
Rainfall in today's morning's coming moments.
The freedom in the wideness of thought,
As is the prison of its narrowness,
Is like being well beside impending malady.
We want to know so that we can govern our feeling,
For feeling is the center of all warmth we can experience,
Yet beside\beyond reason.
If these crowns of surely gold could come together,
And they dally with the full natural a complete season –
Ah, paradise…

Elizabeth
December 17, 2017
David's seventieth birthday

Full Verses

2019 - 2020

Night words

Our hands catch, our eyes hold;
Our hearts warm and spill into words,
Passionate expressions that wield above
Fire, but, more, wishes out needs that
Include all of the every,
And are without any coloration of
Fear.

The wind in the rain took on a song
And left a melody in my thought that was
As sweet as hope in pain.

In memory lies the key that opens
To the ever beautiful.

The past is neither dead or alive,
But a selective, viable bounty of good
And evil, our choice, altogether,
A gift of thoughtful substance, energy – power –
Our choice, altogether: a gift of
Indescribable good to humankind.

We attribute to the moment all of all
That is – and that was – and whether fancy
Or dream, all that can, ever will be – these divisions of
Time, gathering from before in the past, into the
Completion of experience in our
Tomorrows is the reality of our path.

I cannot know, but I feel, and in this knowing,
All of heaven is open to me,
Filling every entry, all pockets, each
Open portal.

The heart gathers and strews,
Its movements and thoughts portioned
Into marvelous vessels of polished
Bronze, to be enjoyed before, after – then and now,
And over again –
The heart does not forget, but
Does beautifully arrange.

Elizabeth
February 20, 2020
In deepest night
One While

The ballroom of a season's opening steps,
Such as early June days,
Finds summer warmth soon bearing
Forth pleasant comfort.
Widest blue above with images in ivory-white,
Punctuated by shining, golden bright
Remind below, fragrances of virile, earthen musk,
Together with resting spring water beneath
A coverlet of patient honeysuckle, fallen.
Ah, come then, maidens, bejeweled and powdered
In gracious, flowing silk,
Flowers appearing within, and finding, without,
Beads and petals, complexioned of all pastels true;
More, pearls of rosen, starlight and moon glow,
As Garmisch mountains' floating snow.
Stepping, stepping into a lane of freshest green,
Rolled out into meadows and orchards,
Filled of ripe confections,
Brought of nature's own: finds then,
Les Memes, les Memes – strolling, strolling,
With gestures and laughter reaching upward –
As the wares that orchards can, allowing to fill purist hands,
The lips of anticipation's blush.
And so, the winds of noon pass over morning,
And in the afternoon, the walk bends to return:
The whole of day looks backward to beauty, indescribable;
Les Memes turn into the path, behind, it resting
On souled soil, the image, metaphor to themselves -
Sweet, and passing:
Before the turn, one while of being, held victorious,
Yet transporting into the bittersweet;
And back the turn, sweet and passing,
Victorious, one while – yet, victorious and lost.

Elizabeth
September 26, 2019
In deepest night, remembering

Reference

This verse can be referenced to the fourteenth century work of Giovanni Boccaccio, *"The Decameron;"* the specific instance relates to the wealthy who could possibly escape the Black Plague ravaging Europe at the time. They escaped to their beautiful villas outside the cities where contamination was more likely to occur. They lived a lovely stay telling stories to amuse themselves.

Looking at the larger meaning of these records, one critic has said (when time to depart the villas arrived), *"The order outside the villas was only a tenuous one; the songs they sang at the end of each day, the delicate feasts they enjoyed, the stories they told pointed to the beautiful preciousness and fleeting beauty of their lives which are too fragile to last, but healing and of great comfort while they do."*

The world outside Florence cannot sustain them forever.

"The Longman Anthology of World Literature," Compact Edition 2008

Beauty of the Passing

To have lost is to come to arrange similar
Thoughts together,
Those which picture the absence of a value;
If the value be dear,
The loss becomes pain.
When I am weary, my shoulders lose their straight;
When I cannot find a treasure,
My hands become useless and when I know
An emptiness that was once full,
My heart cannot find it joy.
Summer into fall,
And the lovely finishing,
And we shout without sound the beauty
Of less with more – but we shout with a sadness
That only fading sunsets can paint.
It is a grief beyond the last coin:
The pomegranate's smoothness,
The maiden's spontaneous laughter.
These all ride the golden chariot of time,
And we wave our arms,
Our hands into its passing winds,
Laughing with its bliss,
Forgetful of the distance passed.

Elizabeth
Undated

Re-weaving

Just now in these quiet moments,
Following days of others, as like so,
I am tender, soft, observing all, so that my
Intuitive whole is a colossal burden,
Surely as the plateau – porch of the cathedral,
Cologne, a revealing symbol recognizing
All of the pain I can absorb.
The beauty of every day is reigning, masterfully,
As the scepter of gold holds out over all;
The past is – lost, but its bounty is more than
Numbers or expressions: tomorrow,
The only true fable, smiles as fine, pouring nectar,
Its flowing meat as a heavy confection,
Its bouquet as love's thought across
The lessening distance.
Oh my heart, draw away the grey drape,
Th sounding dirge, for it breathes
Its first pain out of fear.
Provide a wind which will add strength
To my stance; let light move as a blessing
To my weakened faith,
And open my lips to borrow another's
Direction, leading to a stalwart, firm wager.
Let my courage be re-woven, and take
Away misplaced values on the
Constancy of hedonistic ease.

Elizabeth
February 8, 2020
God is great and generous in His revealing when our needs
Come together selectively threatening.

New, Old Strength

If we could have new, old strength,
Again, would we laugh or simply,
Always, be preparing a smile.
Would nature's movements and colors
Bring us to weep in their first beauty,
The heavy joy of summer radiance bend
Us into thanksgiving.
Could our wisdom be multiplied over,
And lift to waiting needs as innocent birds
Into skyward flight.
Would we not know regret, for
Carrying bountiful weight of recognized
Good, the dark of its sometimes
Good, the dark of its coming
To interment below.
Oh, fancy, bliss, it can be, it is,
For regaining is already ours,
If we allow, inside the accepting
Self of our heart.

Elizabeth
February 9, 2020

Into the Everglow

I cannot know, touch, or intuit
The remarkable joy which sometimes
Bathes over me, a dying radiance
Full in each hour.
Its beauty, smiling out innocence,
Into grave protectors,
Creating a marvelous tension of just such –
How much – yes – what majesty is found
In moments giving this lovely bliss.
Beauty holds a kind of strength,
With the heel aware, andso,
Beauty is more the faire –
Beyond worded description:
Midnight, the gentle gloaming,
The knelling of farewell, farewell, farewell –
Beauty by fated knowing of loss.
Beauty holds what strength cannot,
For thought is ever in composites, yet cognitions,
And there is none, inclusive of these,
If smiling their favor, - in their all –
Which can compete with the joy of ever –
Or the formalized hope of such.
If love is to live, then, beauty must clothe –
The fragrance remembered, the sensation of
Textured silkiness, the sound of sweet recollections;
Together these love in darkened crimson,
Protected veins; - and gracious shadows,
The lightened – petaled rose, muted fuchsia,
And forgotten gold against whispering passings.
Committed to the eye, awake, we, in closing,
Are as the raindrop – carrying its flawless image into
The everglow of history below,
That of now, and now, and now.

Elizabeth
January 10-11, 2020

The Ever Replica

Every echo has its hidden message inside
Its keeping of beauty:
It finds a wisdom, for it speaks of what has always been,
And, yet now, is.
No sunset exists outside it, no honor
Or fealty except within it.
Clearly flowing water, wherever its wandering,
The intractable rock, however composed,
These know their origins within themselves,
The coming to be that which is theirs,
For there is a complete consciousness which moves among all,
Ever other consciousness, and its concrete source,
Arising from the passionate experience of beginning life.
Finds then, what is, has been, and what is,
Will be, if with metamorphic shadings, more of itself.
It is the destiny of all men –
Their gifts and possessions –
To grow, struggle, bear, and to come into one's own,
His individual destiny.
"Checkmate," the final "turn" of the screw always reveal a replica,
The echo of medicinal choice;
Not either of the paradox that humanity is, but the complete choice
To allow destiny which provides the more of the wished –
Rather than vacillating or choosing to accept
Indecision which can yield, but only,
The more of a "*thousand deaths.*"

Elizabeth
September 8, 2019
-another birthday without "*a Thee to love me dear.*"
As per, now realized, my choice –

The reference to the "*thousand deaths*" is Shakespeare's line,
"*A coward dies a thousand deaths.*"

Giving Back

I have come to recognition, again:
Long, long, the steps this journey.
The tasting of each preface is becoming more difficult,
The losses greater, the reclaiming,
More exacting with added, accompanying voices
Whispering "impossible," or "cessation."
But the muse did not "fly,"
And colorful hues will return.
The future will conclude in death –
Seemingly so, presently, but no matter –
The past is not lost;
It remains in a very different face of now.
Beauty is still, and pours out every thought
Which offers to catch.
HolyFatherGod – help me to reach for the baton,
Again, for I feel it close, now, to me.
My only sorrow is that I am not strong enough
To recognize these tortuous periods of growth,
And that they do give back.

Elizabeth
March 27, 2019

Full Chill

I think that I am not ever
Unaware of being alone,
Although it is the seeking behavior
Of my all thought
And movement.
I step and fetch;
I collect and strew;
I am in constant thought,
If knowing all is a paradoxical conclusion,
That choice is more a
Complicated theorem
Than an accomplished reality.
Perhaps I need love, acceptance,
Acknowledgment –
Or an inclusion with few requirements;
Whatever my needs be, they remain unfilled,
And I am alone,
And I know the full chill
Of winter, throughout all seasons.

Elizabeth
September 27, 2019
Just at bedtime

Wovens

Gratefully, we lay ourselves into our rest, the night to embrace our fatigue,
Our spent effort on meaningful dreams, our weeping confusion at understanding –
These constructs given over to the sweetness of rest and sleep.
We, then, on somewise, do not know the fullness,
The grappling with the sands of experience,
Grains into moving mounds, flying by, lifting away, unresolved in awareness
Though somewhere in unknowing levels of thought,
A step was made, a hand touched, a glance caught,
Brimming full – exchanged life came to be.
Blackberry laughter dances about our coming dark,
And soon, the winds of autumn, forgotten for a season,
Begin to refresh our pores, deep into ourselves;
We know, with a weariness, beside a will
Of immeasurable strength, that summer radiance,
Its beauty, indescribable, is as much so, requiring;
And as the infant struggles upward, and forward,
To the man, we feel the cry of mercy at this wind's return.
A measure, a year, is necessary to bring a leaf to green,
And then to yellow or red, into sienna and ochre browns.
In the all, there is an active growing, a casting off, an accepting;
A weaving of chemistry, movement, cognition, and sentiment,
Beside, these come to yield a woven piece, our own.
Wovens offer up an endless variety of the fair and lovely,
Beyond Petrarch's prize, and they all, within a reality. Not all – but more, good –
Active, and resting, if annoying by unknowing and fatigued by waiting –
These qualities, within us, and coming to us, strike dumb
With their pleasure, beauty, and good,
Together with satisfaction and peace.

A bell to ring a school class in, colorful bells announce a Christmas horse,
A distant bell can knell a death; and, out a variety that is truly ours,
Flowers of blue bells can bow, to delight, and our woven is complete, satisfyingly full.
Out our worn gratefulness, somewhere in ourselves, we risk
To somehow embrace the ongoing of the days, for these comprise life,
The space of it we share: ought left is to, in the "*turn,*" "*glory in the glories we have seen.*"
Those of this mind, are shut from all of hell,
Into a separate room of peaceful contemplation.

Elizabeth September 14, 2019
(near midnight, the coming of a new day)
Referencing Dante, "*The Divine Comedy, part, the Inferno*"

Chivalric Review

Rising early into the solitude of beginning light,
I drank in the welcoming quiet
To hear my thought without interruption or confusion.
And the day came in, bringing new discoveries,
Old joys, happy industries, and new reverence for reflection.
-steps and thought in the most pure freedom –
That of self, alone, in Holy Presence –

Trees that reach into the soft blue, above,
Gave direction, and generous hills and valleys bore example.
In place, golden adventures, leather and silver,
Shining in use; andso,
Consciousness pointed to the whole of all,
My now bliss, beside inescapable loss and conclusion –
The elegant robe tattered at inventory.

As a petal falling – softly, quickly, into finishing –
Given, an instructive, perceptive acuity:
Recognition and assessment found eventide:
Rich harmony out hidden choruses;
And truest purity in thoughtful good –
Through the gnawing belly; the bleeding heart;
The hand palsied, the closed eye.

-my heart to nearly burst at the gift of the day passed –

HolyFatherGod, let these heavy tears of thanksgiving,
Out my heart, be acceptable to Thee, holy,
For they have become out of Thy presence, around me,
Within me, holding me, in this moment, in grace and joy;
I am found, now, chaste through Thy most pure ravishment,
Fulfilled throughout this day.

Elizabeth
June 9, 2019
Near nine o'clock pm

The reference work for this verse is John Donne's
"Holy Sonnets," "Batter my Heart"

Entire Matter

I have sat in lengthy silences;
I have lain in thoughtful, deepest dark;
I have stood in constant, pouring rain,
And I have gathered from shadowed windows,
Full preludes to winter's grey.
What of the *"ring of gold,"*
The circle, joined;
All that is, is paradoxical to itself.
And there is no truth in valences –
Minuses ultimately prohibit all else.
Where does good reign in the cathedraled self,
The self being the most often chosen of gods.
Such pondering offers avenues to comfortable
Reasoning until out the god of self stands,
Consciously, the unmeasurable paradox
To full redemption.
The entire matter is too hard.

Elizabeth
June 2, 2019
Early dark

Two Occasions

Please let be, for me, a small,
More gathering of steps in these
"golden, earthly sands."
They have been in place, long, a gift from those
Who brought me to them,
And I wish to wander out,
Their fullest way.
Love shows their path, and images,
Sweet, line their borders;
They are real, and sometimes difficult,
But always strewn with the hope
Of beautiful tomorrows.
Let the refreshment of our small taste,
Together with the huge giving
Of the earth our feet now stand upon,
Bless our hearts this day –
This moment, as if the last –
With this humbly fashioned sacrament of life.

Elizabeth
March 4, 2014
At eventide
-from the record of the Armenian Death March,
WWII, and the verse for Mamma,
Written on Mother's Day, following her
Death in February, (1994):
"these golden, earthly sands –"

Dirge of Day

I conclude, in this appearing moment,
The come presence of a dependent
Remnant of day;
The graceful contours have lost strength,
And thus beauty,
Begging relief to prostration.
Sunlight has become a relentless warrior,
Turning gold into fatigue
And withered goodbyes.
Knowing will allows, still, flowers,
Breath, and memory of ease –
But ah, that the sun would turn round,
That night and darkness
Best Morpheus
Through this dirge of day.

Elizabeth
June 12, 2019

An Hour in Early 2019

HolyFatherGod, how mighty is the fortress
Of Thy Presence: the tender
Fragrances of Thy care.
Give all to me Thy wisdom which I can bear,
And bless all heaviness with the light
Of moon glow and the lifting purity
Of the sun's sterling gold as it rises
To meet the heavens for today.
Pour forth to Thy children of thought
The constancy of the earth's turn,
And offer the unknown glories of tomorrow
To the eager heart of today.
If, in all confidence beside humility,
We can step, and pause in thought,
To imagine the glories of Thy gifts, there is no glove –
The day is ours- there is no contest –
A gift has been given.

Evening

I wish a closing, an intimate knowing
Such as in the words of the shepherd lad;
Let tender care know all about me in these hours,
And bring me into arms as gentle is their strength –
That I will dream of the providential,
Able rising sun, the progress of morning;
The procession of beautiful steps into satisfaction,
The ivory box of peace, at day's close.

Morning

Coming in is a good morning, to be full and giving;
And if not altogether glorious, then in multitudes of small glories –
More, we are in these glories, and we can intuit
In decipherable ways that we are in life:
This construct, in its isness, its being, alone,
Becomes the glory of all things for *"I Am"* –
Aside, only, when looking into the grace of its munificent
Fountainhead.

Elizabeth
Late September, 2019: concluding, five forty-five, morningtime
Perishing Hunger

If there be Presence holding omniscient knowing,
Whisper to my weary soul selected words
That I may hear those of recognition,
Acknowledgement, and care.
Let me hear the unsung melody of feeling
Caught within, seeing beauty in the closed glance
And tender gesture.
And if the sweet, the gold of passion's nectar
Can fill with whole feeling,
Let moonlight touch the words,
And the voice become audible,
That my nourishing dream,
In reality, feed my nearly perishing hunger.

Elizabeth
January 13, 2019

Part is not All

Does summer, can summer somehow,
In its constancy,
Lose its firstness, its splendor of buds and fireflies.
Gathered, first June gardenias are still
Their lovely, their intense, pungent, warm sweetness
Crowding the senses as eagerly rising vapors,
Bringing a glory of dreams and past summers,
As the richness of the most perfect sonnet of love.
But my geese do not anymore fly,
With their familiar callings into my South woods;
The quaint mourning dove has found
Other heights from which to pine his bittersweet refrain;
Choruses of insects are absent outside my dark glass
With their continuously sounding songs –
Lost, lost from earliest hours of knowing –
And the owldove and fireflies make only visits
Of remembrance.
Twilight and eventide, the many varieties of beauty
Found in the gloaming moments –
These come still with the moon and stars,
Hushed by silence:
But oh, my heart, my heart,
Part is not all, and I suddenly find the greatest loss
Is in the unrestrained pining in my soul,
However cosmetically touched,
As it reaches back for the all that has been,
Partially, and without discretion,
Used thoughts and steps,
Usurping the joy –
The dress of innocence.

Elizabeth
June 1, 2019
Eleven o'clock, nighttime

I Feel in My Belly...

In my belly, I feel a sea,
The ill of coming sorrow;
In my heart, I know a quieted fire,
Burnt crimson, the dark of coming loss.
Let not come by me these sensations
Until I have moments, time knowing
Acceptance that they are.

If a Flower...

If a flower can spread its sweetest fragrance;
If the fragrance can collect a softest shadow –
Can we not join hands and bless the moment
Of the all of good.

I Cannot Know...

I cannot know all truth, nor can I see into the center of light.
In self-examination, let me not reject the truth
That purges, that which burns as thorns bathed in vinegar.
Let be that grande happiness find in solitude,
And thought of good –
The wisdom in simplicity of the exquisite Haiku;
The organic symphony of coming morning;
The floral rhapsody of first warmth which early blossoms accept,
The happy sun generously smiling onto,
And the bliss of memory in every raindrop –
That sweet and that bitter –
How then, but that the purging be small,
To bring the glory of waited peace.

Elizabeth
July 14, 2019

Thoughts of Jason while he is in England, but his sentiments close to my heart.

The concierge of Constant Love

Since earliest childhood hours,
I have enjoyed the balming of my spirit
By summer's night sounds.
As much has been my gifting of
Fragrance by the wealth of the Rose faire,
From the garden or the fence,
On which it wanders
Its contented turns.
And when days begin to gather an ambiance,
Somehow, of farewelling,
The loveliness, a distant foreboding,
Would catch the inner tenderness of my heart
So that all of everything painted into all the fullness
Of beauty: a glory, grace, extended, joy too
Great to be lost – as so it surly establishes,
The twilight and once distant seasons
Coming to find their places.
Love, then, begins to draw our wool-flannel
Cloaks close around, and sweet to keep us
That we hold a coming together,
Even in absence, it of natural law.
But the Rose, the flower of thought,
Gathers our expressions to keep into the ever.
Come then, reverned images,
And pour out with liquid moonlight;
Ride about, with sport, the gold of the sun's smile,
And play, happily, with the dew fall in the faery green
Of memory's pastures.

Elizabeth
August 24, 2019
In the moment of midnight
With great love and loss

We can love, yet, as much as we have been given love;
And love can fill up even the emptiness of understanding's
Lack of fullness.

Marvelous Crafting

HolyFatherGod,
Thou had'st dealt marvelously with me,
Thy simple maiden of woods and streams,
Of ever day and night.
I have been given golden rounds
Which cast out darkness and woes,
To gather in the beauty of anticipated good.
Winds come on silent announcements
And breathe into waiting
Vessels of life,
Touching with a garment
Of absolute glory,
The soundings of an interlude of love,
Whose beautiful passions
Leave only an humble gratefulness.
Thy smile opens awareness,
And gathers compassion;
And although often times becoming
Entwined by the rarities, the complexities,
And the heralding majesty of Thy works
Leaves utterance almost impotent,
The heart rests enjoined with the gift of
Thy peace.

Elizabeth
April 4, 2019
Richard's seventy-sixth birthday

-this verse is referenced back to John Donne's work, *The Holy Sonnets*
(*"Batter My Heart"*)

The Reading

The ebbing and tiding of days,
Taken individually,
Or when realized as a larger event,
Constitutes the full wholeness
Of truth in solemnness –
No easier, or more friendly is embracing
The bringings and leavings of seasons,
Or metaphorical dressings of
Sentiments that cover the bliss of morning –
Or the coming adventure of night
Into its peace of closing.
Loss is covered, continuously,
By the forever coming in
Of bright, and forgetfulness waits,
Eagerly, for the moment
Of new assuming.
It is only when we pause,
To ask a question regarding variety,
Constancy, beauty revisited,
Or death in familiarity that
We weep without consolation
The necessity of forming,
And accepting,
The construct that all is a flow,
A repeating of love, and loss,
Of beginning and closing –
All without explanation into understanding:
For the questions and answers are woven
Into each other, without punctuation –
Held by fabled, folded hands.

Elizabeth
March 27, 2019
-the theme reference here is H. Hesse's work,
"Siddhartha" –

The Ambiance of New Day

In the unnumbered, soft glowings
Of yesterday's twilight,
And the twinklings of dew stars at breaking day,
In these are kept the beauty of the innocent truths
Which courted our seeking selves,
That shaped the dreams which have
Contoured our steps, our movements;
Yet punctuating our days' events
Which combined in reason the knowings,
In composite with that which our consciousness
Has tempered, and found, today, in place.
If we could recognize the pirating,
The ravaging qualities of the constant time,
Could we not reach back, lean into,
Embrace with warmth and joy those we were,
In steps which have led us to the selves
We are today, unhappily absent
Of qualities of the constant of time,
Could we not reach back, lean into,
Embrace with warmth and joy those we were,
In steps which have led us to the selves we are today,
Unhappily absent of qualities which
Required the innocence of the sweet poverty
In wonder, awe, and the ignorance of
Adding to the twilight, the dew fall,
The full openness of all that waits in the
Ambiance of new day.

Elizabeth
May 16, 2019

As I Lean...

As I lean into the growing night,
Thou of all good
And plenteous peace,
Wrap Thy coverlet of love about me,
That I sleep into sweetest rest,
Into a portion of celestial
Bright that bides in
The waiting morrow.

Elizabeth
October 17, 2019

Thoughtfully, Without

A glance, quite without announcement,
Diverted to the side;
A smile, suddenly finishing,
In shadow, a voicing impromptu, catching;

A grande cathedral burns, downward through
Its wealth of age, in quickly moving moments;
The mile run, all at once, on ariel steps,
Completed, victorious,
The heart, in ease of life,
Sounding into silence.

Our lives, as dear to us as they are written,
And voiced to be, fare carelessly as we watch
In their portending announcements of passings,
With joy beside grief into loss.

How dear the glimpse in reflection with time's
Appointments – and then so, past remembrance:
Can we feel, truly, *"over again,"*
Or merely find in search of comfort the insight
Of the cutting blade in full,
Hanging darkness, although innumerable
Strikes are ever allowed, given, afforded.

Perhaps we are all as the real Anthony,
Raising our sword to strike our heart,
As he at the bedside of his love's,
Feigned dead body –
"What! Not true?"
Surprising, yet, himself.

-the mind, ever clever, protective-

Elizabeth
September 1, 2019
Just before sleep, thoughtful

The reference to Anthony (and Cleopatra) is from Dryden's play,
"All for Love or the World Well Lost"

-not just strength of mass,
But will of soul,
With warmth of spirit –

Elizabeth
June 26, 2016

-lunch reverie of Richard's final days –

Today found, and recorded,
July 26, 2019

If There Be Presence

If there be Presence holding
Omniscient knowing,
Whisper to my weary soul words
That I may hear,
Those of recognition,
Acknowledgement, and care.
Let me hear the unsung melody
Of feeling caught within,
Seeing beauty in the closed glance,
And the tender reach.
And if the sweet, the gold
Of passion's nectar can fill with whole feeling,
Let moonlight touch the words,
And the voice become audible,
That my nourishing dream,
In reality,
Feed my nearly perishing hunger.

Elizabeth
March 13, 2019

Our Halo, Visited

The fragile butterfly,
In summer's paling gold,
Visits in every breaking day;
It softens our sighs with wings born
About by care, and catches
Our tears in the flow of its wings' veins,
There added to a glistening
Of celestial bright.
Such is immortality gracing us through the day;
And when seasons move in and out
Their places, we are provided, still:
Fireflies defer to the harvest moon,
And in gracious hours,
Berries of wet scarlet
Will laugh into our thought and senses,
Yet prepare us to stand in awe,
And reverence, of purple and rose,
A holy palette appointing chilled skies.

Elizabeth
September 15, 2019

About three-fifteen in coming morning
There is great distance, and skilled effort,
Between a dream, idea – theory
And its become reality;
Most of our steps, cognitive and\or
Behavioral, contribute to,
Or take viable energy away from,
Its realization.

Toward Oneness

Let the humble mantra of my need
Become full half the union of our beings;
"Father, come,
Father bless –"
"Samuel, Samuel:"
"Here am I; here am I:"
Repeatedly, from earthly placings
To celestial calls of favor –
These, over and again, in life,
To bring a oneness,
A sameness of self
And other into good,
The dark in separation coming
To illumining the unknown,
That it glisten as April Snow.
Dialogue into closeness, the laurel leaf,
Anew: understanding and a oneness
Which comes to permit life less of strife.
Those of good heart know hours of struggling,
Fear, and loss – but into
The I-Thou relationship,
That is in continuing with holy others,
Lies peace of man with God.

Elizabeth
July 8, 2019
Near midnight

The first reference (first "stanza") is to *"Holy Scripture;"*
Rumi, the early Turkish poet (dervish)
Is known for the partial phrase (metaphor)
"dark in separation."

Scheherazade of Time a microcosm

It is difficult to live when pain,
In all its varieties,
Takes its turns in expression.
When one's portion has been spent
In unhappy hours in this maelstrom –
Holding energy, and violent winds,
All of the light of the sun's repertoire,
And the night's humble candle;
Knowing the acting and receding ambiance
Of the mercurial fire of passion – confused and laid aside,
And becoming cognizant of truth, unsure and clouded,
To eventually be returned to beautiful fable and myth –
When left with such a ledger of accounts,
These pain and those attending
Within the structure of their place –
Suddenly, the flesh of humanity
Sends out a plea for peace, drawn,
Ultimately, as paramount to all alms that lean into mercy.
And every effort turns toward this grail, and its promising bliss.
Sentiment, in a kind of denouement, becomes, most, a lost echo
Of summers passed, a romance of dreams
And words that do not, cannot approach touch;
Flowers forget their grace, their magnificent hues and fragrance,
These losing breath into the vast emptiness of recognition.
Dark walks the night, sounds speaking their silence;
Memory comes forward, most that of loss,
And joy remembers, the laughter in bitter ironies
Whose thanksgivings emerge covered with
Unsound comprehending of wisdom –
That which cannot hold the flow of life.
The feast appears metamorphosing to the hindward,
One of comrades without rounded purses,
The full grace of friendship; close by,
Camels are chewing in dull monotony,
Circular, wetted sagging –
Into the heat of the left-over day.

Elizabeth
May 25, 2019
Two am into day

To Purpose Life

-a composed breath beside giving truth,
Inside my knowing; one other thought,
Increased, a wisdom of days, a sounding of love
In forgotten quiet; yet a psalm of praise
Out perishing awareness –
Gather to me the roads of memory,
Those heavy with rosen joys,
Pregnant with insights
Already born in time past,
To offer good of ever good –
Open my fatigued senses to the newness
Of elder, waiting beauty, returning winds and fragrance,
Hues that startle in their caught brightness
Of forgiven absence.
And bring to me, to my humble forgetting,
Words that can comfort and inspire,
That can ignite a spiritual flame in their holy rage –
To purpose life – "*in all of life;*
Add the glory of touching love in nearby mortal
Famine, used of its celestial, wetted seeds –
That the harvest of ancient promise spill out heaven's
Truest wealth into a contentment,
Reaching, still, into pathoic struggle."

Elizabeth
June 25, 2019

October Rain

The rain was all day with us,
And I inside its passing;
Grey poured out, beside,
The full that late October
Could provide,
And my verse wept with
Its silent speaking,
I, to receive its dew
Inside my own.

Elizabeth
October 25, 2019
Mid-afternoon

Full Sanctity

In the graciously drawn sanctity of day,
We cannot, but with deep gratitude,
Feel the blessings of new life:
The smiles, the touch, the tender word,
Genuinely, comfortably,
With selfless need, offered,
To then have that which comes into us,
Enlarging the good that already is;
And, to, more, enjoy the bounty of day,
The small details, in their full beauty,
Stored away in the closets of our hearts.

Elizabeth
March 30, 2019
-at full sunrise, though grey, yet:
Jo and Harold, together, into the arms of God,
And each other –

-watersnakes in moving moonlight, secret, darkly foliaged, Persian gardens,
Sands lifting, ever moving, ever still, around Ozymandias, forgotten –

-skirmishes, struggle, full assault – oh God, the forgiving of these bests
Their unknowing; the fallen angels in hell had only their
Weeping for comfort –

The two sources used in this verse, its *afterthought notes,*" are first, "*the watersnakes…,*"
taken from Samuel T. Coleridge's, "*The Rhime of the Ancient Mariner;*"
the second, "*the weeping (fallen) angels in hell*" is referenced back to John Milton's
"*Paradise Lost.*"

This Present Time

-And what of this present time –
The "now" to which I am daily arriving –
Long, idyllic portions of time,
Filled with gracious giving,
Hours complete with moments that gently
Place their wares, briefly, yet brimming full.
Coming in time, also, are the properties
Of wandering dark, discovering,
And remembering all fashionings of joy,
Instructing in loss, and providing ease.
Still is, the exclamation of light,
Its bounty of gold wearing the day;
Its images and colorings, its details of wisdom;
Its monuments becoming, the full worth
Of the far side of triumph.
As lovely as the pear and pomegranate,
Together, are the qualities of patience, and discipline,
Unto supporting, giving, preparing and waiting –
These arms – kept – from cultivation
In living poorly, and well, these exercising
Will in brambles of circumstances, dissonance,
Fatigue and the camelian of esteem.
Andso? If "silver" and "ruddy" become descriptively
Acceptable, how grande in thought,
The enduring truth we can enjoy –
If the thought can go the distance, all the way out,
And remain with its verity:
We, then, celebrate the antique castings,
The concertos living, still,
Sounding the heart's most sincere sentiments,
Marvelously held in time.
These courtesies become as words of care,
And offer content which lives past the unexpected,
Feigned glory, and the absurd whose premier
Quality lies in its being forgotten.

Elizabeth
June 12, 2019
Near eleven pm

A Moment in Night

Night is everywhere, yet crushing
My inside rooms;
Rainfall comes tender to the ear,
But distant in touching ease.
Why does the heart feel despair in
Circumstances which suggest
The solemnness of truth, it in heaviness,
Not to move other than to punctuate its message.
All know well, and always,
To gather our rays
About our sentiments, to look, and see, to know.
Nothing is a lonely island of thought,
And with its emptiness,
We can but thrash and flay
Our knowing self –
To fall into suspect,
The full of all knowing.

Elizabeth
June 4, 2019
At bedtime

-alone with reflective hunger, wishing to know
past this moment –

True of True

Walking through is a beautiful effort,
Strong in strides, and weak in pause;
We reflect and mummer that all together
Is a part of the whole, and we forget, cover,
Replace or, in some fashion, do not know
The full pain of repeated loss.
Such discourse is not fullest wisdom,
Taking away the depths of feeling with which
Our souls are often filled to bursting.
These simple explanations are true only in a kind
Of diminutive truth, in perhaps the security
Of another's speaking, offering almost
An arrogance in feigned strength.
The sentiments of the heart, whether felt briefly, passing-
As a response to a glance, or for an exchange
Of greater import – these are recorded
In sensitive knowings whose meanings may evolve
In the particulars, but the full understanding will bleed
Through time, and the seasons it encompasses –
As kept – as the searching in a familiar review,
Or as faithfulness finds the pale tint,
"*forgotten*," in the rose's dust of many
Summers, slipped away.

Elizabeth
March 23, 2019

-"*true of true,*" *even as the faded rainbow-*"

A Dying of Much,
A Birthing of More

Love in its fragrance of lingering twilight,
Its passion in sweet struggle over its still giving embers;
The remembrance of things past,
Shadowing the coming night –
But the reality of effervescing dew,
The wisdom of the living sun,
Moving into its western dim –
All is still and yet, the touch of warm,
The sound of tender,
The knowing of a togetherness –
In every awareness, a glory,
In every cognizance, a giving,
How much in the moment, knowing,
Yet the glory in the glories that have been.

Elizabeth
August 18, 2019
Rising early, afraid, but in gratitude
Six-thirty Sabbath matins

Reaching, clasping, giving over to knowing –
Afterthought

Coming Day

Coming day reminds the beauty of light,
One of the true glorys of the universal,
Existence, being, precipitate growth,
Then decay, these dressed in lovely seasons
That cover the schedules of our
Steps in mortal dust.
And more, light is instructive,
Illuminating our thought that we create
The wealth composing our true
Significance as we walk
"these golden, earthly sands."

Elizabeth
June 12, 2019

The closing line of this small verse, again, references the
Very personal sentiment I hold of my Mother.

I Am Being Given Back

A spontaneous smile within the night
Becomes a jeweled scepter,
Held out, reflecting, sponsoring good –
Its igniting thought, a crown,
Yet its glory.
In the betweenwhile, the morning sun
Waits its birthing worthiness;
And night rogues come to hide,
In their unhappy ventures,
Falling to golden appointments
Of sparking light:
Fancys, smiles of new day.

Elizabeth
June 27, 2019
In deepest night

I am being given back, in smallest pieces,
In abundant thought.

The property of paradoxical thought, and will to examine it,
Is the fall, conclusion – the tragedy of the construct of
Peace for the human intellect.

Ungiving Solitude

Bramble, bramble, coquettish twine out,
Tuffs of dust-laden tumbleweed
From its wandering,
Together with blowing, brown paper bags,
Soiled with wet, joining.
Quietly, they all, comrades, - all – my unspoken
Awareness burkes my will.
How can I not consider, more,
The elegant emeralded moth to wed
With the scarlet flame.
-not a name given the flight,
Only an adventure into peace,
The bliss of giving solitude;
The taking, the exacting –
The perfunctory press, always,
Of lacking – these
Having been satisfied.

Elizabeth
September 2, 2019
-difficult holiday, alone,
Only because no one knows-

Lay Me in Thy Bed

Lay me in Thy bed of sweetness
And sorrow, to be bathed in joy when
Dark comes into morning.
Let fresh pearls that dress first
Roses halo all the sentiments that wait the day.
And if my portion fall a gift of seeming less,
Grant abundant reflection
Of happy conclusions.
For this is the way: that these
Properties draw their balance from the all others,
And we stand, in conclusion,
In peace.

Elizabeth
March 28, 2019
On waking –

Just in Advance

Just in advance of daybreak,
Finding myself near to the dark
Of the kitchen window,
I saw lights of a vehicle, traveling
The periphery of my east woods –
Small, innocent, moving –
Seemingly – fancifully,
Of their own effort;
Gentle, soft –
Almost mystically
In beauty of their own stillness –

Elizabeth
July 23, 2019
Eleven-thirty pm

Time's Monument

It was beautiful when I found it;
And my fatigue, great,
When I embraced it,
Althewhile dubious in its capture.
Now as I touch its meanings, its truths, and beauty,
There falls a sadness, for it speaks as a memory,
Not the glory it possessed in arriving, for
We tend to darken our elements of the past,
Distance them as we reach, again, for
Their worth including many properties.
Ah – we cannot ever know that which we
Have known, caught in thought, recorded in words –
Not the first, full sentiment which
Pressed to be scripted.
While we process in enduring to our over- full
Self, we lose, and as close as we
Can, again, come to gather, is in recollection,
Sweet in a somewhat darkened halo that stands
Monument to time passed.

Elizabeth
January 22, 2020
Eleven pm

– a tribute to the glory of the experience in a moment,
the beautiful loss of time past, and the sometimes' efforts
to recapture –

Images

And in the night, I found broken glass,
Reminding eggshell turns,
Half-moons of shadowed light –
These in graceful fallings
Across my shoulder.
And in the night, I caught the
Early winter's cold,
Joyful, inside, its warmth of wearing.
Could be these images very waking blessings,
Calling out of deepest self, a true
Demanding of their awareness
In reluctant wakefulness.
Ah, beauty court my thought, always,
Bringing all thy beauty sweetness of innocence;
Pouring out my distant realms of thought,
Signaturing all good, in sparkling,
Dew light meadows, flanking
Standing halls, grande; with
Winter berry scarlet against
Crystallized snow:
These so written in flowing, darkened –
Giving peace.

Elizabeth
December 14, 2019
In deepest night,
one forty-five am, quiet …

Kept Rosen Gold

With his passion-driven sweetness,
He left to me an image
Filled of life, to be,
In always, the felt of carrated remembrance,
It to bear light of love, exquisite,
Begging as long as thought is long;
The beauty of closeness that usurps
The mortal and finds
In peace the bittersweet of
The heart of touch – immortal –
Rosen - golden thought.

Elizabeth
December 9, 2019
Near bedtime

– of Ross, speaking with Becky

If Love Could Be

If love could be love, without being love,
Perhaps such as holy prayers
Of gracious saints, lifting;
Or the window of a first raindrop,
Opening sensuous thought and touch –
All the nothingness, the innocence pure in concept –
Such can, in very perfectly designed,
Honorable moments, become sweet bliss –
Oftentimes spoken of in jest,
In feigned sincerity, in power and, perhaps,
In myriads of sensual hues;
With most giving, which rarely can be
Objectified, the bliss that can evolve is a
Fashioning such as one which can wound the heart.
But surely, as in redemption, it can –
It will – grant the bliss necessary for life
Of genuinely giving, becoming much as the grand
Motif of the concerto in entering
The glory of its flower.

-the bliss anticipated – is the flower – its becoming, the opening-
It become – the isness.

Elizabeth
January 30, 2020

Afterthought

Our hearts are more capable of finding feelings that include
Behaviors for engagement than our reason is always able
Or willing to enter into; sentiment does not see\feel the collective
Whole\path of reason – long way from idea to reality.

Second Afterthought

Life is only, and all, arrangements of love coming together,
Pulling apart, to again come together with the original pattern,
Or one, most times, very much like it –
With sufficiency enough to keep a troth –
Be Eros, Agape or other –

Full Verses 2018

Summerlude, 2018

It is a kind of truism that of beauty,
The more it embraces an entity,
The more of it there is –
Not just in measure –
But of itself, for its intrinsic
Being is increased.
The property of beauty
Is a long-sought quality
Because it is, by its nature,
Its true essence, good.
To add simplicity to the arrangement
Leads to the ease and warmth
In beauty, without complexities and distance.

Andso, behind are lovely words
Of lovely arrangements
Which share, with ease and delicacy,
The whole beauty of good:
Wisdom stands alone in its first strength –
Beauty in truth.

Elizabeth
July 5, 2019
Evening's closing

The reference, in the whole of the verse,
Is the philosophy of the Romantic, British poet,
John Keats: *"Beauty is truth, truth, beauty…"*

Soundings

Silence, silence, bound by stillness,
Flowing, flowing into the leaning glow;
Coming, coming, surly, now,
The truth of reason without
The raw of its props.
How to bear, how to not know –
Press, press close, promises already given.
And if the promises already falter,
Let wisdom come, to count
The substance of the hours.

How much I want to be brave, strong,
And to push into the bramble
I cannot truly understand –
Back, back, indolent Morpheus,
And let my spirit rage;
Perhaps some truth will out
Its confused knowings; let its sentiments
Flow into hearts that bleed for wisdoms which heal,
To make the conflicted, broken –
Whole again.

Elizabeth
Undated

Ah so, the day had been long,
And in its slowly passing moments,
Almost completely silent.
But as the sun dresses its palette of evening colors,
Sounds are remembered,
Those in lengthy paths, those of the newest evening –
For in the away these again begin,
Bringing joyful surges to encase my whole –
And I smiled –

Heavenly paths are, always, and include us
When our hearts need warmth;
Ah so, the night will be lovely in its giving
Length of darkness.

Elizabeth
August 19, 2018

-after bath, following a quiet day,
Almost speaking harshly to me, at times –
The river which fails to catch the rising
Earth pushed for a time into the open soil,
But in its given hours slows
To only wetness and no flow,
Into that become the dry earth.
So I feel in this moment,
Slow from the fatigue of drying flatland,
In no fashion able to push into flow.
Needing a repose of a thousand years,
Then to feel rainfall, I need rainfall,
I need reason, hope, and faith,
A psalmist and his words else I,
Though a queen, eat grass with herds.
How can – what kind – of refreshment
Can be ministered unto me
That I catch the memory
Of my salvation.
The care of prayer,
The strength of the bow conditions
To wield relief, to stay until
All energy is restored and faith
Is whole again.
And when moments come that
Are barren of thought and utterance,
"pray Thou, Thyself in me."
Lord have mercy;
Lord have mercy;
Lord have mercy.

Elizabeth
First week of December 2018

Being alone has not ever appeared
Such a reality as this moment –
In my bedroom, inside continuing rainfall:
Unseen, unheard, away
From all thought –
And still I feel, and most,
Aware of the properties which seal
My isolation, alienation, my barren;
Yet, I am not near death
Or being crushed beyond accepted life;
I feel, most, myself,
Accepting without judgement.
My physical self is friendly,

My thought inviting;
My sentiments are quiet
As if in preparation for touch.
How does a being know such content
Without the introduction of another:
His dreams are faulty –
And no color appears that is lovely
Into perfection.

Elizabeth
November 23, 2018
"*On Love*" having just been read, from "*Musings*," p. 100, 2009

Wounded Peace

The day ended quietly as the night
Continued its forgetting;
Time was again alive in light and shadow,
And the clocks posted their bringings and takings.
Awareness became at once a stone of great beauty,
But a reality which pulled forth heavy sounds
Of unfortunate knowings.
The paradox in fuller knowing brings together
The tenderness of humankind.
We rush and wait, we hope and fear,
And we gather and strew.
These steps let us see the oneness of us all,
And we come together to weep
In a wounded peace.

Elizabeth
August 13, 2018

Let my voice sound above
The raging storm;
And let my fingers know
More in touch than those
Which guide the unseeing eye.
Spread throughout my whole,
Forgiveness, as the malignant canker,
Destroying flesh that is
Caught fast in hurtful wishes.

We are unbound need,
Seas of wishes, gowns and jewels
Of selfish pleasure, knowing so
But not aware.
Let the stone roll backward
On all evil descriptive,
Crushing every cell of temptation –
Or let the heart of intense sentiment
Pledge to will and faith
To fling the stone to perdition
On reaching the crest, leaving us free
From a portion of predestined grief.

Hail Mighty God –
The serpent is caught,
Bound beneath the stone's
Surface, touching

Elizabeth
2018

Darkness embrace me and offer
To forgetfulness all that I know.
Give me the hellish peace of Dido
So that I carry my hurt knowingly,
Without using it up.
Peace always sponsors a wager,
And mine was lost for want of more.
Freedom is bound by its own pleasing
Philosophy, and those who dally in it
Are crushed in its bringing.
As the grey webbing
Of smoke leaves its passion in the earth,
Call a wind to come and take
All away, away to an eternal
Repose a freedom which gives
And takes all –
Ah, darkness work your wisdom
So that in knowing nothing,
Wanting nothing –
Having the all of last
Be my final peace.

Elizabeth
Sunday eventide
November 11, 2018

Within and Between

I move within and between,
Together, touching and without knowing;
On my bed I dream in absence
And a sense of loss of that which was.
Do others know their loneliness,
The singular self who understands the passing
Of moments, the ordinaire,
And the unfamiliar.
Does championing the self increase its reality,
More into a worthy being whose fullness,
Whose isness becomes greater?
To stand alone is at once brave,
And more, the less;
Togetherness bides not only acquiescing
But standing stalwart in reason;
The wider self needs more, balance,
Than an extreme of stance and motion.
Andso, I beg to the flower,
In radiant standing, and finishing dimming:
Give to me, in touch and distance,
The fullness of the both.

Elizabeth
May 5, 2018
Bedtime ponderings

The Passing

In most an ambiance of still softness,
Days pass, and we conclude that time is in us,
Was in us, and has worked its paths
Through dusts of gold
To the now of that we consciously know.
Bits of tedium, struggle,
And sorrow found their way, if,
To the brevity of thought,
Only a small pasture –
To the side, perhaps, or pressing from behind,
But softer, than the fore.
Leaves of purest hues shadow
Out the necessary sunlight,
The radiance of first flowers gracing
Every step, and as from the perusal of gentle ladies,
Fresh fruits fall to their waiting glory –
Sweet and remembered.

Elizabeth
Spring, 2018
The inevitable

Dream Pearls

In dreams that are true,
Over and once again, we know their pearls,
Their beauty, and unkind witness.
And in early morning moments,
They wage war of heavy truth against that
We cannot put aside;
Andso to the wanting self, beyond
And deep within, leave, please,
A place for just a while,
And let bide, beside, a knowing of good,
That far away gives from the dark,
And comfort enters,
In company,
Of the lovely and kind.

Elizabeth
August 24, 2018

While contrast is still a valid construct,
And early spring's beauty sits
Intermittently beside left –
Over, winter grey,
A sadness – and is easily close by out thought,
For cognitively, sentiment draws there from.
Sleep, the "*little death*" so once explained
Reminding of this such reasoning –
Restful, completed, restorative behavior
We all must insist upon,
But a kind of acceptance of a reality
We do not understand or,
Truthfully accept until pressed.
Much akin is the lovely Christmas stocking
Of a home, once alive with bright,
Novelties and activities quick and joyful;
Joyful still – but shadowed by the ash and mists of times,
They, clouding the colors,
Their creative properties to the self
That is not fatigued with steps.
We are not gods, but we wish immortality

In all of its many gifts we conjure into being;
Ought then we need fill each moment's
Experience with all fullness possible;
Ah, moments: they come and come,
But pass, therefrom, and are not
Just so ever again –
We must, then, gather moments
In the instance of their realization.

Elizabeth
2018

Beginning Again

There is no Thee to love me dear,
No sweetness to wet my barren dry;
And more, there is no presence
With sentiment to embrace my ever feeling,
Reaching emptiness.
Such realities present when Spring,
In earliest appearings,
Suggests such absences,
Shadows of other hours of night
And early morning.
Images and details of physical properties
May enter almost as apparitions
But emerge as fully beautiful aperitifs,
Promising moments of savory
Recollection and giving feeling.
How though, as the mirror comes to show
The perfect image, with every corner lighted,
The day in its fullness draws our place:
Dew fall rides the sun's smile to its lord,
Petals forget the brevity of the hour
Of their rarest bud;
And winds, early mornings matins,
Gather warmth in coming hours,
To take away the perfect breath of fresh, new day.
Reason works its magic with fancy
And the beauty of expectation
And familiar findings acquiesce to time;
And left is, yet_still_another glass
Of golden wine, truly rarest
Nectar married ultimately to its stem.

Elizabeth
March 7, 2018

Responding to early hours of Spring
If a blessed plume with its heart,
Wet of full joy in the beauty of the earth;
The warmth of camaraderie;
Yet the sweet of love –
If this flow can be exchanged
With another – heaven's bliss abides.
But if the plume, dressed in ebony,

Issuing its flow of a darkness,
Its heart full, wet,
Reaching from pain of agonies
Such as loss, neglect, unacknowledgment –
Taunting words that sting,
And poverty in all, by love of none –
If this darkness can reach another's such heart –
In understanding, and accepting –
Benevolence, grace is.

Elizabeth
December 11, 2018
Eight o'clock pm

The wealth of pain has been for my heart, my yearning soul,
The opened purse of falling pearls.

I Want

I want to hold all of me in one knowing,
None left behind or yet to come,
All washed through the present,
I want the one construct we are incapable of internalizing
For more than the eternity of a moment –
That of perfect balance –
The moon is in its down just now
And appears a glorious star –
How like our perceptions of all in this matter of *"balance and me."*
We cannot bear inequities of self and must weep
Our own inner knowings,
To reach again, and always, again.

Elizabeth
March 13, 2018
Early rising, five o'clock am
-the eternal difficulty in living is resolved through the words of the Ancient of days
Luke 6:31-38

In This Now,
Come Lyrics of Day

We are alone, but truly, together with God,
In every step of the stones laid out,
And those all within;
To be is to endeavor, cognitively,
With a self, aware, knowing into finding,
To be full of joy in our being:
Coming into a holding of true good,
Washed over so that there becomes a completeness,
If with pain.
Confessional conversation poured out the heart
Arrives the self not any more unclean.
And with this coming of conscious grace,
Power and glory fell to the earth
Around me, like golden claspings to the good;
I wanted desperately the lyrics
Of the day to begin.

Elizabeth
July 24, 2018
Three-forty am

My most need is every quiet/all in none;
Circumstance is so obstinate,
Quiet the challenge to will.

I see coming a window,
Out of which lays down
A pasture whose green bears
Every touch of beauty.

In the radiance of day,
In the peace of night;
We can know God, briefly –
Intimately – that God is -ever.

Elizabeth
Undated

Three Sentiments

Somehow, in shadows and bright – God,
With me – we have traveled from
The beginning of awareness
Into comely and gracious pastures, in time,
Those passing into holding beautiful moments.

Begun in January, 2018
In a quiet moment of reflection

Suddenly, in grand mania's perceptive insight,
I embraced all to me,
The surprising excitements, the disappointments
And inconsistences, the loses and memories.
In this moment I was filled completely,
The palette newly furbished,
To paint out all the glory that I can absorb,
For in reality, there, in truth,
Is more than the reality perceived.

Hours alone, those in deepest night,
Pressing close together,
Hours barren, of much exceedingly emptiness –
But immeasurably, bountifully filled.
The contrasts in life offer it with greatest wealth,
Through paradoxical tension,
Expectant of joy.
Mystery and legend, fable, a narrative glorious,
With divinely decorative appointments –
The "*survey*", wonderous and giving.

Elizabeth
February 22, 2018
The word "*survey*" is referenced back to the old hymn of Isaac Watts
"*When I Survey the Wonderous Cross*"

When night is come, fully,
And covering, I look about to the day,
And small vestiges of its face politely
Smile to me, quiet,
Shyly against the majesty,
The fullness of night.
And knowing the hour approaches

Which turns away steps and thoughts,
I look about to the safe passages I have.
I often wonder from which knowing
I catch the confidence, the courage,
The hope to embark on another journey
Across the deep.
I smile into the darkness at my
Misinterpretation: my faith is far less
Than ever enough,
But it rests on Thy immortal
Arms of Thy love.

Elizabeth
October 21, 2018
Just at bedtime

The past will ever travel roads
Which press our softness
With tender pain.
It finds corners and shadows,
Wind that sings, to appear at times
As a frightened guest to our waiting hearts.
Its color is always grey, punctuated
By the adorning splendors of our own,
And we grasp these as confections
Which could melt away in the heat
Of our discovering joy.
How humble the Adams that we are;
Mighty God, give us words which
Might describe our gratitude
At serving as husbandmen,
Both day and night,
In Thy garden –
Beautifully complete –
As we taste the golden nectar
Of Thy love,
Within Thy thoughtful
Benevolence.

The architecture of my hands is unhappy, my hair silver;
Ever yet I trust, in joy and fear, to see again Creekside violets
In their king's royal purple, to kiss their freshness, held,
Of the early morning's dewfall.
November 2, 2018

September birds in September sunlight,
These in afternoon playfulness:
How shadowed juxtapositions
Show as the bright of autumn reflects,
Sending back to the radiance of summer.
Now and ever in kaleidoscope fashion,
Colors spar for permanence as they
Pass into each other.
We cannot hold, but rather gather,
With giving energy,
For beauty after beauty is all the more
Exquisite in its entering
That already established.
The all of it is a solemn beauty and grace,
And we are more within
Ourselves to have it come to us:
Early, and late, then and now –
Today, tomorrow – they are as one
For they give and take,
Beauty and its gifts,
To ask back again when we
Are richly filled.

August 3, 2018
Early afternoon

Time Left

When there is no time left,
Time again is given with expectancy
And youthful joy.
Questions are of little, true concern,
And the evening is yet a
Waiting fable, promising a gathering
Of recollection, soft ease,
And satisfaction with what is.
The "why" of the realities laid out before
Is no more than an exercise in able thought,
For the moment, precious in its being,
Washes into a bliss that leaves no room for
Conjecture and dark.
"Haste, haste, make 'aste," –
Words from hearts before who lived and felt
The absolute necessity of bringing one's
Whole self to every gift of light.

Elizabeth
January 4, 2018
On waking, eight o'clock am

Providential Gift

When sitting in the earliest daylight hours
Silence as full as a presence,
Thought ventures forth, to quickly return
To a more comfortable setting.
Fully aware consciousness awakens
While allowing other levels
Some residual space – and we find that
Late seeking thought insists our attention:
Much now is, so much so
That it is with difficulty, and sometimes pain,
That we be led to a knowing of the
Center of being.
Perhaps out the center a golden,
Flaming candle of truth will sing its song;
Perhaps the Lilacs in the dooryard will, in
Beautiful Spring cadence,
Again express ultimate truth;
It may be that the brilliant cobalt blue
Background of last season's Azaleas will mirror
The riddle's hold on our hearts.
More still, perhaps these all, together,
Will answer our pensive soul,
With every other phenomenon of good –
For the riddle is not a splendid
Turn of truth, but a door wide to the heart –
To look, to listen, to touch and think –
These into the joy,
The providential gift of the feast of life.

Elizabeth
February 4, 2018

The night rides on heavy hours
In the darkness that is my only company:
And adding reason to my sentiment –
Such has to be, for there is no oneness to gather into onliness.
Such is most of choice, unhappily,
But a forced choice, since in ourselves we ponder
And bathe in self-absorption,
Ourselves, most-alone –
And this behavior in its loneliness
Burkes the voice, the whisper,

The almost weeping need for another to touch,
To breathe in kindly knowing
The emptiness we suffer to claim.
I cannot know differently, or more,
For the beauty of self-examination turning
And becoming prepares its pain into recognition,
To, in a become sense, the beauty
Which is as the blooming flower – complete –
If ephemeral, laying down its spent self for a return,
A coming season of renaissance.
What matter, then, the dark.
Beauty fading is beauty becoming
And to seize its process bests the prize.

October 18, 2018
Alone and in the knowing, understanding, human pathos
Two-fifty on Thursday, coming

As God is Good

As God is good,
Let the day pour back into itself,
For it has been dark and silent,
Chiding and heavy,
Only outside the smile of every
Wished-for portion.
Grant a fullness come in the night,
That tomorrow smile,
As do all tomorrows,
And the joy of the feast be found,
Full, again.

Elizabeth
June 26, 2018
Just at bedtime

Three Comments

One

Innocence, and dreamt, half knowing,
Early hanging pears wrapped in gold-speckled bronze;
And partially blown, while fully giving,
Fragrant roses – ah, the being of youth,
At the understanding of these realizations:
More, again – now – into ever.
We plunder our sentiments and reason
With clocks and calendars,
Making successful thieves of time's wealth,
And the glory of our whole passion
Soon to be diminished
Into suggestions of shadow and weeping.

Reference above to my favorite German "romantic" poet, Holderlin
(pears, roses and such)

Two

-to seek, to somehow know – enough – to make amends:
So good is God.

Three

Andso, rainfall on early spring green and multitudes
Of colors appearing like birds
Lifting into their lighted flight;
Joyful to seek the day and its glory –
To press to or own the luminance,
Somewhat, of the glories already seen.

Reference to "*Dante the Divine Comedy, Part the Inferno*"
An anecdotal observation: all is more than it should be, as is,
Less companions sweet with whom to share, to divide, to give.

Elizabeth
April 3, 2018
Just at bedtime

I cannot know all truth
Nor can I see the center of light.

In self-examination let me not
Reject the truth that purges,
That which burns as thorns bathed in vinegar.
Let me find happiness in solitude
And thought of good,
That the purging be small
And bring the glory of peace.

Elizabeth
2018

In the radiance of day,
In the peace of night,
We know God, briefly –
Intimately – ever,
That God is.

July 27, 2019
Two-forty am

Bye the bye, the hours passed my way,
And bye the bye, sounds press unheard;
By the bye, the shadow, the rock of being,
Casts its fullness over me, all,
And so, I know of existence, alone,
Of Thee and me with conversation within
The shadow of the rock.
There is awe and mystery, hope and fear,
Joy and peace of the emptiness
Of giving and receiving –
In the complete loss of whole gathering.
How so of this filled emptiness –
Yet lies in the hour of willing acceptance,
Of the weight of the rock,
Yet its shadow of peace.

Elizabeth
August 26, 2018

If I Could...

If I could bare feely the soul,
True, that I breathe unannounced,
Winds would, on every corner,
Whisper gently; the sun,
In all his majesty,
Would lean forth, forgetting,
And flowers would arrange in the rarest
Glory of the dew-fallen morning.

Elizabeth
2018

When I awakened, the sounds were all of quiet,
As dark is within every point of without.

Healing, healing, with every fiber of my own:
I was mending.

Elizabeth
July 24, 2018
Three-forty am

Anguished Cry

Silence, silence,
Bound by stillness,
Flowing, flowing into the beaming glow,
Coming, coming surely
Now the truth of reason without the raw
Of its props.
How to bear, how to now know –
Press, press close, promises already given.
And if the promises falter,
Let wisdom come,
To count the substance of the hours.

Elizabeth
September 18, 2018

Full Verses 2017

and passing

Yellow Carnations, fully exclaiming
In the morning's four o'clock;
Reviewing penned thought into coming,
Their glory captured in a moment,
With pleasant sentiments to the side.
Can we hold the necessary when realizing,
Becoming cognizant of the present instance –
Can we yet find the requiring of self-discipline,
To enjoy the golden spontaneity that is ours,
Then, alone.
Reaching, holding, knowing in past moments,
Revisited: does not time merely redress
Its trappings to step, again,
Into itself, giving us a stretching out,
The unbounded glory of spirit inside giving,
Continuing awareness.

Elizabeth
June 16, 2017
Four o'clock am

A Psalmist's true revealing –
June, outside, in deep south Mississippi, is glorious,
Surely a taste of the fabled heaven: ours to know, to hold,
To keep as the passing touch of love to seeing innocence –

To see and feel – the wait of faith:
The only constant is God

Seeing to Know

We do not carry a mortal eye,
Nor that, either, immortal,
But sleep and wake with open thought,
Alive to Presence allowed to us.
Like a dusty carousel, we move round,
And through, spheres of joy and sorrow;
And with our thought,
We spread hypotheses into theorem,
Explanations pitiable, but somehow,
Comforting.
And when our steps no longer make the dusty
Print, and the *"fleshly"* eye *"sees"*
Spiritual realms, we merely perceive more,
And differently, a continuation in *"alteration's dress,"*
But, yet, familiar, the self.
Angst need not stand our constant companion,
For it is out of the feared unknown;
Perhaps we need conjure nothing,
Save to look to see what is.

Elizabeth
In deepest night

-moment of hard reality-
After the "snake incident" – must make decisions:
A dark hour, before light –
Four o'clock am

-so far to light, whatever the circumstance-
Undated

-a Shakespearian influence, here – *"alteration's dress"* –

The Poacher

For many, perhaps most,
With the exception of those finding themselves
In, then, shadows and greys of life –
And recognize the persistence of the hound –
For those greater most,
Death is like a poacher, shy,
Knowing the balance of his steps,
Yet deft, agile, to the mark.
The hunted know of their circumstance,
The young and strong,
In a romantically flowering ambiance,
And the old and weak,
More stoic and resolute, for all are,
In this reality, innocently aware, yet,
In wearing the shroud.
In reasonable appraisal, through the wealth of our
Growing consciousness, we, then, wander,
Seek, hide, and, in scholarly fashion,
Pour into the riches of worded thought,
Drawing intensely, the mask away from the truth.
Would the world be more beautiful,
Our sentiments, sweeter, passion of growing,
Even into heated fury without this threat
To our always innocence; perchance not, for alertness arouses,
And makes bold detail – may be –
The riddle approaches the intuitiveness
Of the "*eternal questions.*" And with no answer possible
To our faculties, we are left to live it,
Groan in its incisiveness, its complete lacking of any forgiveness.
The fallen, brightest learned of the creation fable,
When just fallen into hell, and in indirect evil,
Began the hunt. And so, we are here arrived.
Ah, poacher, be the stealthy soft, be quick to the mark,
For we in innocence, in the hunt, have already been
Wounded enough into a fearful surmising,
And intuitive knowing.

Elizabeth
December 11, 2017

Behind the Veil

Deep, Mediterranean purple, with threads
Of finely spun gold;
And all about it falls a shadowing, to rippling,
As the light of stars, the flashing of a wealthy smile,
Around a golden and leaping, demonic flame,
Becoming a rubied glow:
A darkened veil hangs, before, and thoughts
Collect hours in reason, wandering
Away to struggle, waiting, before, behind,
And beyond, in a questioning of all time;
As we arrive to its presence,
We wish to lift the veil, but it requires,
Perhaps, more knowledge, strength,
And courage than – any, each – of us can be assured we have.
And if courage is in poor repair, possibly a vision,
A voice, or a prayer will begin its inventory.
We are of divine fashioning, but cannot, without commitment,
Go beyond a hesitating avoidance of responsibilities
Necessary to accepting; it is this arrangement which brings,
Into semantics, confusion; prayer offered,
Personally, leaves, therefore, despair,
As the drape refuses to fall.
The thought leads back to presence in mortal flame,
And mortal angst multiplies –
Like a candle burning into a pool of its own self,
To eventually die; we find a world behind
With theoretical rose – responsibility to only, again, surmise.
We, then, become afraid or our acceptance,
To beg grace, as when we find
Understanding of our whole self.

Elizabeth
June 21, 2014
-on passing into sleep, thinking of the whole matter of death;
The script was almost impossible to understand,
Possibly because of denial and of coming knowing,
But most, the press of fatigue, bringing sleep –

Admonishing Shadow

Shadow, shadow, yet absent thought –
Into the distance you find me,
Still: grey, with light of varietal intensities,
And, then, away with no pattern of returning.
Wandering images – asleep, awake –
Leaving a heaviness, or more, a compounded
Fatigue which bends and bears open to let fall my
Precious coins from my purse of spirit,
Into an unbearable emptiness.
Beauty is, still, but it is separate to itself,
Not touching, neither receiving,
But must to be sought out, and howso –
The fatigue and its press,
Inside shadow that does not review its grey
Beside its lighted spaces, that a balance might be foraged.
The unmerciful, and pretender to peace,
That awareness is, yields a journey wide and rewarding
When its host is tolerant, malleable and accepting;
Yet the issuing of the flow itself calls urgently,
Pleadingly, for the hem of a garment whose reality
Is of many textures, its presentation clear of a confusion of choice,
Its origin and being with noble lineage and credentials.
Shadow, shadow, dim into the away,
And let whatever is left to clasp and carry hope –
Let, please, it to be kind.

Elizabeth
A very difficult day which has accomplished a kinder
Conclusion, if still perplexing –
September 11, 2014
Near midnight

It does not matter the distance of the lies
You spread out to my knowing,
Nor the emptiness of the sentiment
When gathered in.
Nor do the flourishing, other infidelities
Cleave my heart, but rather the gentleness
With which I was made to believe,
Trust and hope.
A smile here, a touch there,
Soft laughter in comfortable climes –

These rose up in me a certainty of troth,
If always unspoken, in asides
And clever unsurities.
And in this circumstance lies the
Great sorrow of my heart:
To know that Thy appraisal of my whole self,
To be so diminished,
And continued in place so long a day,
Like holding up a mirror,
At each sunrise, to my – to Thee –
Inadequacies, in my soft courage, out believing love –
In this circumstance of perceived smallness,
Incompleteness, confused knowing –
It is here that lies the heaviness
Of my unrequited, constant care.

Elizabeth
In deepest night
June 21, 2010

Of J., our long togetherness that was only an empty hour
Stretched out, with colors that were, at times an apparent true,
But to quickly fade to barren other –

The mornings come in with their joy beside
Their ever reminders.
All that has been touches with gentle certainty,
As do suggestions of expectant hours of the unknown true.
Difficulty in contentment lies like a used fair linen,
Beautiful in reverent must doing,
But knowingly, a lived in reality,
Speaking the passing of time,
The ephemeral face of the beautiful.
Blossoms left to the side in childhood's innocence
Within the discovery of morning's new glory:
Comes death to every moment in its inception –
How lovely, and sweet and, more, how lovely and sad,
The pathos of all the aware.

Elizabeth
December 23, 2017
Four forty-five am

On waking to gentle rainfall, aware of the *"everlasting arms,"*
But with a heavy sigh in the awareness of the
Beauty of this blessed season –
Soft rainfall, truly blessing_

The trees are becoming old, casting off; I sleep into consciousness,
A coquette in presentation, but truly into a sleep awake.

Does fire always, in its trying,
Always purify,
But rather, without justice
Or mercy,
Consume.

I am old and tired,
And my remaining, insistent fire
Finds an impotent vessel
In which to burn.

The heart cannot but weep
At a moment's close,
The bringing finally of the complete
Roundness of orange freshness,
Into a wrinkled masked fop;
The cheek of the pomegranate less than
Her true rose, the day's goodbye
At twilight, knowing again, more
And more the aching aloneness in my, now,
Impatient soul, one of fewer days,
The more the wish of love to come.

As the bird flies into tomorrow,
As leaves quiver in soft winds,
As morning is born in simple, seasonal waves
Of quietly coming light –
Could not but love of good passion
Lie gently about me.

Elizabeth
October 11, 2005
Early morning, at sunrise

Rediscovered "Nice" Lines

Only "acceptance" is full, if, yet, in emptiness,
And brings enough, even beside our dreams.

In haloed moments, when pleasantries fall about
Like luted pastoral scenes, to face futile
Unknowing is only a cloud
That passes between us and the warmth
In sunlight, a coming aperitif to
A sweetest cordial, of standing, full being
Inside small belief.

Silent rose of rose, leaping emeraled bamboo;
Fullest skies draped of constant ivory –
These hushed into our personal solitude –
Thought in this company offers a repast
To unmeasurable hunger.

Elizabeth
Spontaneous fragment
At twilight, March 17, 2012
Transcribed March 11, 2014

First Awareness

At the first awareness when toadstools
Become creatures with hues
Of pleasing sensations,
And vines and tendrils move their way
As steps of the able dancer;
When the chorus of light crescends
Into recognition,
We pause to think and know,
Our true nobility;
The echoes of being come forward,
Again, and joyfully,
With the great saga of resting into passion –
Together, fairies, sylphs, and playful sprites,
Their ariel qualities manifesting
In catching the dew fall's counterpointing,
Jeweled lights –
Oh, glory, into glory –

Elizabeth
On waking at coming daybreak –
May 2, 2014

The dark is past, and light is generous
In its blessing;
The *"many miles to go"*
Assume a joyful cadence,
Steps in our dusts
Of time enlarging our very
Given significance.

Elizabeth

The phrase *"miles to go"* is from the modern American poet,
Robert Frost, *"Stopping by woods…."*

Sentiment, One

Thou had'st my heart
In such sweet bondage that I would
Gladly come to show to Thee,
So, but because I am bound even more
Than these words, said,
I would not, less to exclaim
The full of my sentiment, aware.

Elizabeth
May 13, 2018

Divine Architecture

Life does not leave us – ever –
Only to pause, perhaps to rest,
To re-engage and continue so that all
Possible thoughts and feelings
May be experienced.
That we do not understand the particulars –
Yet the constructions;
The pathos of time and yesteryear,
The splendor of a morning dew fall,
The softening day into twilight –
These only are understatements
Of divine architecture.

Elizabeth
A "verse" while breakfasting
September 28, 2016
Seven ten am
At home, Elizabeth House

Inside my first awareness,
I want to run to you, run to you,
To chronicle the night when you are not there,
Except in beautiful, unworded
And knowing assurances –
To speak of adventure in the coming day –
When laughter and all good play about.

But most, to know, again,
Once again that you are, and in our fashion,
You are with me, beside me
In touch and smile,
And understanding,
Across the miles reality strews out,
But close in sentiment, gardenia sentiment,
Early summer warmth
Sentiment that is ever within.

Elizabeth
June 7, 2007
On rising

Empty Gatherings

When small particles slip away,
Unnoticed, within the scattering of all,
We find with gathered moments,
That something good has sometimes been lost.
The full breaking of day,
And its attending refreshment,
The movement toward purpose, and fulfillment,
Into familiar fatigue –
And the joy in beginning again –
These, unhappily lean into a pattern,
And we reach, in concluding,
With effort, only to find,
Often, that of the day,
That pleasingly quaint, the simple,
Lovely diminutive –
Or the strange and instructive –
These have become –
Empty gatherings to our hands.

Elizabeth
Undated

Can I Bear Thee

And as in first consciousness, loneliness swept
Over me, being somewhat the moonlight
Moving through moonflowers.
The sentiment did not stay other than
A distant dream, a very true visit
From my mountain; and in those reachings,
It occasioned brief tears for all of the
Absences inside my beggar soul:
Love evolving, farewelling, holding; beauty,
Must to be fulfilling in dying,
Through its tenderness;
Hope, thoughtfully, lost;
Triumph, passing, hued of revenge, and yet –
The excitement of first chartreuse.
Were there angels in light;
Apparitions in white: the bolero of roses
Weeping in warm, twilight dew fall;
Where are the swans of graceful circlings –
A falcon, a tower, an unsung song –
Consciousness and awareness are enlarging,
And the moment will not be long,
Not the angels, not the swans, the unsung song –
And sweet the balm, but oh,
Pure radiance of sweetest pain,
The vehicle of truest knowing of self.

Can I bear to wish Thee come again.

Elizabeth
At twilight

The Mourning In Early Springtime

-early springtime, garlands of iridescent beads,
A spirited pantomime of blossoms in cold winds
Of old Provence; an innocent glance,
Aside, finding three, small violets;
My mother's hands, opened into my grounds;
A late, yesterday afternoon:
A visitation from the past of ever presence –

And in glance found a tenderness,
An old hurting, a secret wound, a beautiful
Possession, its acknowledged mourning
That spring can offer, as an olden mead-like nectar
I drink into its each such appearing.
These findings pose a painful glory of the season's
Beauty, a prophetic glory, outside its bounds,
Into the remaining cold and bare,
And coming sunsets, still,
Painted in hues of purple and rose:
Seasons passing each other,
As lovers in a new awareness,
Entering an appointed chambre, that they come
Together to fill up each other's absence;
To, in a completeness, gathering
The only left of the nightingale's roses,
To find a complimenting, a new oneness,
The very essence of all yearning, searching, finding.

Creek side violets, small and delicate rose-blue,
In springtime, felt in childhood's always innocence –
Into a noble consummation, yet a foreboding
Of the known – coming, and necessary departing –
Found in the heart as shadowed,
Yet sacred loveliness, emerging in time,
Over, and again – not unlike a waking,
An impromptu intermezzo –
Upon its arriving.

The Embracing

At the time of first light,
The morning came in on heavy sandals,
But full dew fall was, still, yet –
And cold – first, frozen cold, the morning
Finding fresh vigor in bearing itself,
For it bore in gracious beauty.
Its quietness found almost a sadness, a kind of
Homesickness; shadows, however,
Chose to spread kindness, and moved into
Their most, their unobserved, absence,
And, in clarion gold, the sun cried out the glory of life,
Despite the covering of winter's bare.
Into the day, into thought and sentiment,
Both together brambled with routine and dreams –
Fancies, hope, and delicacies of good,
Companioned with confections of passion,
Although the radiance of summer smiles,
Now, a fable, remembered, insistingly, warm.
Constancy yields strength in its faithful everness,
Comfort through seasonal pretendings suggesting,
Always, a tomorrow –
"Our tomorrows glory our present,
And hold in awe the wonder of reflected will
Inside time, past:"
The always process of orienting.
How but – in cold and still –
With secret needs, very burdens to be kept –
The grey wine is in its season –
How – but to struggle, marvelously,
Into the wealth of the gentle beauty of the Pleiades,
Bright: to stand – before lying –
To rise, then, into the grey,
And embrace the wealthy bare.

Elizbeth
December 10, 2016
Near ten o'clock, pm

-winter: a very reality, at many levels; words, lines, and ideas taken
From my work, "*Seasonal Portions*" (2012) –
In the Russian Orthodox Church it is custom to stand in re-
ceiving the blessing of service (entire).

Holy Scripture

Job 29:19

"My root was spread out by the waters,
And the dew lay all night upon my branch."

And I dreamed of blood sausage of many days
And dry barley of small wet, and sour,
So abominable in taste and sentiment that the image left
My altered consciousness where dreams
Know their nativity;
But so powerful was the fable that leaving,
It was not forgotten, and reached
The consciousness of objectivity, a reality
Of thriving nausea.
HolyFathergod, prepare again my root with
Thy waters, and let the dew lie all the night upon my branch:
For in seemingly unknown steps,
The blood and barley of our days have become
Dry unto death and foul to our inner selves.
Grant, again, once more, the moisture of Thy Wisdom,
That of complete love, to bless in renewal,
A very renaissance come in the daylight given,
That we become fresh and fully able
To know the beauty of ourselves and others,
To flow as a river, spreading our refound
Breath of sweetness.
Without love, in its many guises, our behavior
Becomes decay, as left blood sausage,
With barley, small wet to sour,
To be placed, together,
Into the castaway.

Elizabeth
October 17, 2017

Can I be, come to know...

The breath of frost in my chilled window
Gave out to a surprised glance –
Snowfall, small rounds, and stacks, paths
Leading away into familiar cereal,
Brown leaves and broken limbs.
-and birds – with energy all quite unfamiliar –
Southern snowfalls are rare, and there conjures close
About a kind of mystic aura, of happenings
Not ordinarily known:
A time of beauty, a time away from plagues,
A time of passing, and ultimate return to our once.
I know the origin of snow, its very breath of beauty,
It wandering away into the very well studied –
Large, yet, grande; but the mystery remains –
It is Winter, and I do not know the wisdom of Winter.
Green will follow, and radiance, with figmeat flesh,
Dressed with its scarlet veins – these into the gold of harvest,
More golden ochre, to again, more of Pauline silver-white,
If bedecked with shrouds of dust;
-but from where – and where to – why anywhere –
Why: gather the metaphorical larder, extend
Conceits in their complex loveliness,
The elongated, wandering – finishing –
Alexandrine –
But can I be, come know the wisdom –
In the long of cold –
Of death to life.

Elizabeth

The deep South does not (as per record) sponsor heavy snowfalls – just enough to be fanciful and pretty; the reference to the "plagues" is one of the recordings during the "Black Death," the Bubonic plague, which almost devastated Europe; the figmeat is from my father's plant in summer, "yellow ochre" an embellished gold, oil paint. The Alexandrine, a technique used by the author of "The Fairie Queen," Edmund Spencer.

I beg in reason to let it die to me –
All, all that no more need is to ignite any ash
Of that before.
Punish hindward thought and burn in flaming smiles
All which leads back to former days
Of hurt and loss.
Let me know the peace in unbounded freedom,

The joy in selfhood as fresh as Springtime's
Full spectrum of images, and in this new strength,
Let me hold resolute and undivided.
I reach, eagerly, for contentment, that not leaning
On such which can only ask until I am
Left emptied, more barren –
A self, weakened and filled of fear.
I press toward fullness of grace, lifting up
On Thanksgivings, and trust to don garments of wisdom,
Having scales let off my eyes,
Together with gathering weeds of Samaritan
Covering: and, added to, faith of the ancient fathers
That I will live in the joy of the all
Good of others.

Elizabeth
December, 2017

Christmastime, 2017

The season comes to draw, again,
Itself, into a blessed fullness,
To purse on time our memories of the sweet and good.
White, seedless grapes, colorful commercial
Fruit, and chocolate still linger
As distant images, but with intense sentiment;
And a togetherness that cannot be bested
By time – for the heart does not forget.
The past is because it was.

Elizabeth
December 21, 2017
Six-thirty am
On waking, among tender musings –
A very glory

"Thou should hide them (they that trust in Thee)
In the secret of Thy Presence."
Psalms 31:20
Holy Scripture

In the peace of early gathering twilight,
In the softening of mighty winds;
In the acknowledging smile of the passerby,
In the music of truth out a studied psalm:
Blessed is the peace in the secret of Holy Presence.
When friends are most, circumstantially absent,
When out the bramble of the dynamics of kin
Issue emptiness and questions,
When lost verses begin to whisper,
To fully voice as at their first –
And when the summer Rose blooms in its own again,
In November's chill:
Blessed is the peace in the secret of
Holy Presence.
If darkness does must to gather,
And loss shall must to surely be;
If joy can only wander the rainbow's path

And fade into distant echo's hues;
If acceptance is ought our only having:
Blessed is the peace in the secret of
Holy Presence.
Thanks be to God.
Amen.

Elizabeth
November 12, 2017
Just at bedtime

In reason is a simple, holding truth:
Opposites always companion each other
So that the balance in being may continue;
Andso, when cold within dark must speak out
The gold of harvest, before the brilliance
Waiting in first spring green –
If we can find ourselves in place
Of cognitively understanding that our
Sentiment be another full –
How blessed is the peace in the secret of
Holy Presence.

Elizabeth
2017

Small Islands

Great thanks, and much praise for the small islands
Of respite which hold in place,
All along our earthen way.
In morning time, there is the open window
Which surveys the wide of sky,
In virgin white, seafoam blue,
And the riddle of teal, in fellowship with the good
Expanse of earth, showing browns of sienna and ocher,
With spritely blades of green,
Sponsoring laughing berries.
In night, moonlight streams the circumference,
Natural softening and making clear
The unknown dark, the specters which
Are housed within.
And, washing through our thought,
Whatever our hands find to task,
Our steps to engage,
The wealth of reason embroidered by
The details of imagination and fancy –
These gifts come to sit beside the reality
Of the moment – its finding and its loss,
Yet its seeds of glory.
Blessed are the moments of such gifts,
Cast about into full harvest,
Sending out their gold to the
Abundant joy in being.

Elizabeth
December 24, 2017
Flowers, bright, suns and moons of all the celestial, and comrades
Who do not fully know or understand the guises we don –
These do come to take or hands, and our hearts,
And lead us, together, to table.

Ruminations

I need a psalmist, else I eat grass
In the field, a queen demented.

September 1, 2016
Dated much earlier, but found again,
and transcribed this morning
four o'clock am

Where did I lose them to,
Moments and hours, sensations
And abiding sentiments –
How much of life we throw away to the
Unaware, small perplexities,
Unknowings that will never touch.
Hesitation too often becomes master of rich impulse;
And if denouement, then losing is the best forward –
Sweet in its review, and promise of another –
Perhaps – more.

-a mushroom cloud of fantasies – indication of loss of that left –
Objectivity, wished?

HolyFatherGod,
Come inside me and satisfy my needs;
Fill me up into a very harvest.
Amen

All of early September, 2016

This afternoon

The afternoon is long and the muse is kind,
Bringing worlds of thought which engage joyfully,
If painfully; the reaping is, happily, in its whole,
Golden – white, and I am more content.

-some lines undated, but all of late August,
Early September, 2016

One Morning

I awakened suddenly, the timepiece
Bursting with frenetic voice,
Seemingly within every corner of the room;
As cognition unveiled the morning darkness;
Despair in all things seized my heart;
Silence spoke with its thousands of ringing bells,
And I knew the old dilemma,
Much as the youth in his early seeking –
His pursuing, adventuresome thought.
The supporting of a fatigued will,
However, led into grasping about,
To find the fabled summer,
To pain and beauty,
Know the pathos of crowding reality.
The darkness, the stillness,
And within the unspoken message, also,
In all of morning –
These came together to find a peace,
A strength in a reservoir of hope.
The day began, again, its lament of jaundiced gratitude –
Steps, bramble, dust,
And faintest light.

Elizabeth
November 12, 2016
-on watching the day come in,
Five-thirty am-

-out one of my, of late, "seizures," of doubt, fear, despair –
Inside the establishing ambivalence within the knowing of the,
Still, beauty of life: ah – Hamlet –

Waking Thoughts

Because of seeds and stones interned
Through years of forgotten steps,
I can find but trust in this remaining dust,
To live, into a wish of each day past:
A fold of safety, where thought,
And fellowship in fraternal peace,
Midst reverence, spread inside benevolent grace.
Every sunrise in its gentle glory,
Draws distance to every need of Eden's larder –
To a presence closer to peace, through,
But beyond planting, striving within green,
To, past its radiance and absolute joy,
Into harvest gold, entering denouement, and,
Beside the disc of being, descent and still.
Yet, within the moment is all of now,
A gift beyond properties and measure.
The glory of sunlight is gifted another once,
To give without fealty,
Ought gratitude and its footmen.
We can carry all of ourselves, all of the lighted hours,
Into all portions of our wait,
The blessings, and the peace, to lie down
Beside what struggle has been required,
Yet allowed – the unsaid wager somehow fashioning
A geometry, beautiful, if only in being.

And what of passion: it lives inside, pulsating to
The movement of every good.

Elizabeth
October 17, 2017
Three-thirty am

Bounded Heart

Bounded heart, held without movement
By decrees of reason's more complete wisdom,
Can the true of such arrangement arrive,
Verity's true.
Deep pain cleanses, and darkness
Yields one humble; emptiness holds forth
A golden carriage filled with shining expectancies;
But the pause in reaching holds a sword
That bears complete, and unbounded.
I fear that I am left to become torn into great
Cleavage, left undone with my own.
Warm, warm, and fresh – my blood pours forth
My own; as deep as Scarlet's velvet drape,
It holds my every care, the senses
That have brought complete joy,
The reason holding all in place –
All in place of my own –
Lost of any and all of the verity's pure.

Elizabeth
July 16, 2017
Sunday afternoon, long way down
Reference in this piece to John Donne

Fullest Anecdote

In all fullness, I feel my glory,
The dark of night, the secrets of my heart;
Fasting smallness, embracing the complete;
Let contentment remind the joy in accomplishment
Of the unknowing, love with it small
Particles converging, to become in the fore,
To proclaim a victory over all love –
Though it be beyond measure or description.

First awareness, and the particular bent of
Consciousness, leading into an ambiance which
Can offer everything or nothing –
The bridge or the abyss –
The very gift of every day –
How not, then, fullness, glory,
A decided contentment,
If musings, aside.

The dark of night, the glow of sentiment –
Portions of the divine, and their magnanimity –
Incense, vapors, seances – these become
Anecdotal to the prayers
Of the knowing self.

Elizabeth
September 18, 2014
Three forty-five am
A good day passed – if closeness to the inside
Of pain and fear –

The whole of life is the greatest
More than I can think,
And the agony of/within its wealth
Pours me with my tears
Nearly into the pit of death.
Still, still, I cling, I reach, to clasp
Its own, mine, my own.
Great, immeasurable the combined
Contours of the heart's crimson.
To love, to lose – to,
In reviewing farewelling –
Such is surly death in thought,
The piercing pain of absence and dark.
My signature fades, and I am left;
Andso, clear, clear, the
String's voice in press,
The violin's joy sounding
In the pain of giving flesh.

Elizabeth
July 26, 2017
Just at bedtime

Unnecessary Maneuver

So seems now, each night, a need
For long preparation, for expectancy of that I do not know,
Ought but the surety of dark unknowing.
And with certain reason, so I find the morning,
Its waiting familiarity which wears a foreboding –
A caution – with furtive backward glances, almost a reprimand: to launch out,
Even into prescribed waters of appearing calm.
Still, more, the fall of the golden lord,
In his fullest majesty, so that the afternoon wanes
Long, and reflective: full toward the loving, giving angst of twilight.
To assess our hours, days, and years is a fearful
Venture, in all, a selfish maneuver,
That we emerge as we think we ought.
We weep as children over time past,
Its losses of many seasons, its unrealized dreams,
Its holdings that were ours, only to slip apart, their warmth left
To us in synesthesia and thought.
Water flows just such, on and past, with its goods and without.
The sun is above a small while,
As the moon floats in waters dark, briefly toward the day.
Ah – Master, in beauty is truth, and "all we need to know- "
We go, then, eagerly, comfortably, so to our mat,
To lie down, to rise up, to be busy in the betweenwhile,
To know there is no maneuver possible,
For there is, in wisdom's reality, pressing need.

Elizabeth
November 30, 2016
-written as I approach December 1, closing another year –

The conclusion found above is not in quick resignation, but abandonment of selected will
To misunderstood truth: beauty in all. The stupor which becomes a self (inside it coming
Into being out intense searching for a sterling certitude), such clouds
the "spitzer," so that the day, all truth, is forfeited.

The reference to "Master," is to the, perhaps, most renowned British poet (the "Romantic Period"), in his verse stating his philosophy of life – *"Ode to a Grecian Urn:"* *"Art is superior to life."* – or better said, the spirit fashioning the work holds a portion of the beauty, objectified, that becomes the only immortality of it we can know.

And What?

Unexpected reflections in sepia tones;
Laughter out forgiven hopes
Of innocence; pushes and shoves,
Ignited by bursting joy –
And joining, the leaf falling, beside,
Quietly being, with a menagerie of flowers,
Their softest petals, contoured breasts –
Lying against each other;
Colors of flawless sky, wearing all over;
And berries, behind – these beginning the early,
Sweet imbibing of passion.
Thought stretches, falling back on itself –
To right, again – ah, beginnings are beautiful –
As complex as closings are painful, simple, and true.
The gift of now; only momentarily,
It serves with the fringe of innocence –
A gorgeous portion, verily, surely –
Of us *"lesser gods."*

Elizabeth
December 3, 2014
Wayne's seventy-sixth birthday –

In a bursting of recognition,
I find myself alone, alone,
And childishly, fearful –
Fearful of crowds of demons which,
In canine pressing, bark and hiss,
Throwing about, bellowing their threats,
In a heavy mist, dark and swirling.
Their presence is close, running the inside
Of my thought, my imagination embellishing
Their strategies, memories punctuating,
And fears of the intuited, waiting, but unseen.
The plains of Carthage appear,
In these moments, more real than before,
The battle done, fires dying,
Smoke, now almost a friendly fragrance,
An aphrodisiac to sweet images –
These lifting above the silenced reality.
With every awareness of myself,
I stand in agony of seeing,

Of loss and losing.
Truly, however, I am one of all,
And as the script is written,
I choose, most, the station of warrior;
With true tears, I accept my dress
Of appropriate loss.

Elizabeth
"Loss dresses every warrior"
We Lesser Gods: Addendum (2017)

-the calls that cannot be allowed;
-the words once whispered not to ever be heard again –
How do I bear these absences,
These emptiness', yet filling to bursting
In their sounds of reflection.
Early summer is just in, with Gardenia
And rose, long, visiting light,
And thoughts which awaken with each jewel
Of the first stars, each soft
Wind that speaks, a portion of beautiful
Ambiance of this present,
Sitting even more beside.
Ought to do but savor Camelot, to hold
To the warmth of it yet, to know
That we carry the present, we hold close
That passed, and we journey into their tomorrows –
The one gift we have for a season,
It filled of smaller seasons,
Their color and substance very gold.

Elizabeth
May 24, 2017
Early evening
Pensive moments

I heard early morning birdsongs,
Fresh and jubilant,
And I thought *"they do not*
Know the kingdom is coming,"
For them, at hand,
Their day closing a nearly finished season.

-So effortless, how without travail
They sing their psalms,
Beautifully in awe of their cosem
And its mechanics.
In the quieting of their calls,
I heard a gentle reproach:
They have always known of their day,
And their season, and still their
Songs are such that they ring
In a constancy of the wisdom of acceptance.

Elizabeth
2004
Buttressed
-Feathers, in brilliant colors, and those showing in brown and grey,
Rose within sounds of worship…

Within Silence

Each moment of silence that falls away
Sounds as words of lamenting verse,
The dark melody of the dirge,
The petal's gentle struggle to depart its centras;

Yet, the kaleidoscope of yesterday
Within the turnings of thought,
These against the very despair of soon approaching,
Beautiful eventide, inside its
Beautiful evensong – the words:
Farewell, farewell, farewell.

Elizabeth
February 7, 2004
Could it be that life, is truly, but a wait, on the wings of the wait of faith?
-To leave, to part, to farewell to the gathering for which,
In our patience, yet is unseen.

Completed Sentiments

Forgive divided faith and moments
Of despair; accept what steadfastness can
Be in the guise of weakened clinging,
To become enough for fullest joy.
Bring together these divergent qualities,
Knowing the all munificence
That completeness is of Thee, all of Good.

Elizabeth
2018

Grant us peace, not in repose,
But in the feast;
For all can gift death,
But only of Thee is life.
Indulge us with the bounty of
Thy table; let us find peace
Of slumber, dreams bright in darkest night,
Hope born of our lineage
Out Holy Loins,
Celestial birthright.

Elizabeth
2009

The Mirroring

In fullest consciousness, my sudden waking
Found a wall of silence, that of the fallen hours.
Those of the birthing morning,
Its travail without voice,
But speaking as a torrent of images
Surging about, a very floodwater of festival
And memory, into the halls of yesterday.
And I do not wish to journey there,
To wander among the voice of my solitude,
Its quiet bittersweet,
Its insistent absences which dress with
Emptiness, certain chambers of my heart.
-To paint out shadows, to allow echoes to die;
To sound chimes with bells,
To press old flesh – in these would
Find mortal my solitude,
But, in these, almost, without a saving reprieve_
If these chambers of absence should
Fragment and fall away, leaving me,
In greatest truth, but of complete fullness, less;
And so I must, beside my laughter,
Provide a mourning, that the whole of me
Leap forth, full awake to day,
To stay its hours, let hanging given,
Imaged in form and fragrance,
The rose, nourished by its own, emptying,
Mirroring the full bittersweet.

Elizabeth
November 23, 2003

We forget, yet we remember, in stances
Different with the years; and in moments of quiet,
In seasons of special significance, images visit
In their real and metaphorical forms,
Having metamorphosed, but also having
Kept the heart's own.
The stage remains the same, for we live yet,
If between different props, but the players,
The script and its scenes continue to arrange
Around the deeper parts of ourselves;

So ought to do is but to catch
The beggar coins that fall from their purse,
And hope that they add beauty to the afternoon.

Elizabeth
November 24, 2007

To be alone, how to fill,
To cover and tidy when alone of the gifts
Of voice and touch,
The ear to presence arriving –
Not at all except in fancy and memory –
And so the sword pushes, with force,
More into deep, still, then:
For they either never were or were known
Only to could have been,
To come more to my heart,
All left, to my heart. Thou winter sleep, provide
When dreams die or be born
Into the unhappy circle
Of distant knowing.

Elizabeth
October 1, 2003
Cool tonight

And I am, again, alone, still

Magnificent Fancy

The reservoir of yesterday, the isness
Of the moment, the promise of tomorrow –
These portions of what has been,
Is, and is to be – real – are –
I think, a magnificent fancy,
Like wished for snowfall that covers
Waiting thought.
Surmise would, then, that I bejeweled the flowers,
Fragranced the winds, and,
Out my consciousness, the great mystery
Whose origin lies in shadow –
Out this consciousness, I drew a feather,
A then become lighted torch,
And touched the eastmost sky.
There enters presently the poignant
Beauty of yesterday, the radiant, only of
Today, and expectancies as a thousand dove,
Set loose to draw tomorrow.
The real, in felt sentiment and worded truth,
Becomes more a fluid construct as our steps gather,
It ebbing and tiding in unending flow,
Out to its lost fountainhead
Which embraces neither bejeweled flowers,
Nor fragranced winds, but only
Knowing that something distant was,
And now, it all, ever is.

Elizabeth
January 7, 2007
Five-thirty am
-thoughts before sunrise; soft rain, difficult moments –

Silent Knowing

Give us small moments of silent knowing,
To clasp, to hold the full bliss of tranquility
Which smiles out constancy.
As in the flowing of water, the progression
Of the grande motif, the rhythmic struggle
Into life, let us somehow feel the absolute power
Of grace – through all manner of unbelief,
Reason and the forgetting of our true natures.
Bless the seed given in our unawareness
That it flower into the fullest
Wellness we can know, that we find
Strength, while reason,
And the power, the courage
Of sentiment to be receiving of all joy.

Elizabeth
August 26, 2017
In a small moment

Yet and Still

How to say, how to carry pain
On the embroidered wings of well-chosen words,
Those whose arranging create an ambiance
Of beauty and goodness through rapport,
Serving ease. Yet and still – dark
And hurt can become heavy weeds, lifting about
Through which the weight of a spirit's
Breath is drowning in the nausea of wounded soul –
In these vessels of sentiment, we live and die,
Hours out wandering days –
And not so much in lack of courage,
But in its torture of carriage.
Sighs, and their accompanying, whispered
Breath, are beautiful, in either
Their glory or ashes –
But ah – the true is that, more often than sun stars,
The golden pear's blossom of fragile ivory –
In autumn – or the cardinal red of the master
Bird, in uncommon circumstance –
More often than these,
We perish in the tender grande of our glory.

Elizabeth
July 13, 2015
Early afternoon

-thoughts, and wandering mood, pressed by the realities
Of held fancies, and the clasp, yet grip,
Of the world – inside, and the outer must –

-the world of "*dinga, dinga*," (things, things) of Rilke, the now
Becoming most renowned of German poets (yet Goethe);
Rilke was early twentieth century and lived a very "unordinary" life –

The Become Rose

The Fullness of the Thesis Statement

"The Come Rose"

The thesis statement has been made, and discussed in the, perhaps, most efficient manner: through description out deserving examples: the theme finishes with all thought that is strong enough, true enough, and lovely – becoming the rose which has journeyed out its hinterlands.

The final verses (roses) which follow have been gleaned primarily from the work I have grown into expressing within the past two or three years; however some of these verses date much earlier, having made their way despite very little time in their adventure. Dark is no constant, only always reminding – paramount to all such discussion sings this air to all time: light is majestically perpetual.

(verses chosen date from 2001 – 2020)

Elizabeth
January 24, 2020
In afternoon sunlight

In my belly I feel the ill
Of rising sorrow;
In my heart I know the
Emptiness of coming loss.
Let not come by these sensations
Until I have time,
Time knowing acceptance
That they are.

If a flower can spread
Its sweetest fragrance;
If the fragrance can
Collect a softest shadow –
Can we not join hands
And bless the moment
Of the all of good.

The malaise, spreading the peacock
Of pathos –
And, always, the hunter,
Fancied, given able to strike
Over and again into my will:
Why do I, yet, run,
Woundings aside,
Only knowing.

Elizabeth
November 12, 2002

Fragment out
Deepest Night

-gone with the wind,
Its bitter to return on the wind
Inside of sweetness;
The balance: leaves…in their constant
Movement find,
Without saying –

Lose to find, again,
To know, again, loss;
-unlike to clasp, again,
In the reaching halo of forgetfulness –

Elizabeth
In deepest night
June 29, 2015
Four-sixteen am

A remembered melody,
A forgotten voice;
The wind just so passes through
September – how do
We hold these beauty long enough
To enjoy past tears.

Memory, with all of its properties,
Enhancements, with distance,
With hope and joy of our present needs –
It cannot ever approach its resting source;
Indeed, truly it cannot,
For it was not ever the once we give to it.

-tears, tears fall –
To become knowing if,
Unapproachable;
Beauty – all time –
For we are, in truth, bound.
I heard sound in the outside night,
Much as such old women dying,
Slowly with their horses,
Until vehicles in the still,
Dark distance made sounds with their
New day, humble
Chariot rounds, singing –

Fragment, undated
Spring, 2017

Sentiments

Felt words, spoken
Are eternally kept,
These so written, the full blood
Drops of one's
Soul.

Elizabeth
Early Spring, 2017

Continued Sentiments

And we gaze into the beyond of
The looking glass mirror,
To, in its depths, a full,
Fiery glory see:
The scarlet blossoms of our thought,
The sweetest dark our thoughts can be.

Elizabeth
November 26, 2017

Thoughts of W. B. Yates in the recent night
"silver apples of the moon, golden apples of the sun"
(paraphrased)

Ah —

The night, and alone,
The sky above me, the colors
Of seasons and the bright
Of the sun,
On water – these to my senses,
Alone – and I,
Present with my left-over
Dreams, alone.

Afterthought

Let seas mirror the good
Of the land and hearts sing the
Melodies of the wind;
Let hands each to do good,
And thought be agile, clear, seeking
The universe, positive, complete.
For a season, beauty is ours –
Can we pour over questions whose
Answers offer no peace;
Let the storm in living be seen
As a prelude to first light,
The expected comfort of safe refuge,
The proclamation of joy
In living.

Midnight Prayer

-God is good to all, touching His own mightily –

In the night's exact midnight hour, I asked my pen, on waking,
To sing my song.

I thought of you often, over,
Quickly, wishfully often, for it is in our
Fancies that lie our true realities,
Those our hearts know though our arms
Do not embrace, and our steps not to wing
Towardward, our eyes open onto.

In that hallowed portion of ourselves that is feeling –
Knowing, sensing – finding holds the very
Essence of being, and playing out is only shadow inside
A season, not the eternal song of the ever self.

Raven and chestnut, agile and lathe;
Innocent and aware, able into giving, into being;
-natural law beginning its unravleling,
To find its unknotting, lost –

Elizabeth
June 15, 2007

Ever Image

A vacant lot, a street beside –
And on their stems of bush-like green,
A legion, surely,
Waved and tossed their captured
Sunlight to me;
And I held once again childhood
Golden-rod, these in now,
Under the year's last smile,
Hauntingly lovely,
Autumn time.
-Interludes and preludes,
And where the moment:
Silver into green,
Green into silver –
Autumn time.
-And so.

Elizabeth
September 22, 2003

Morning is coming –
Little rounds and squares of light,
Their jagged, shadowed edges
Slowly melting into widening glow:
Flowered sprinklings of the select commodity,
Begging like rainfall, to appear in
All the scape I can see:
Everything is gradual, portioned,
Segmented, though altogether beautiful flow.

Elizabeth
June 6, 2009
At sunrise

Patience is the connecting, the building thread,
As strong, in the strong,
As bleeding scarlet.

A second white Calla, spotless, flawfless,
As pure as it sisters the Magnolia
And Gardenia, making a rarity in these
Early summer hours, found only
In their fashion, in our summer climes –

Prison Aware

The tenor's flower opened, again and again,
Falling about the moments
Of darkness inside my rooms,
And all the colors that ever I knew
Spread forth as snowflakes in reaching hues;
The sweet fragrances of yesterday
Blew as sweet winds across my heart,
Riding the glory of bouqueted
Laughter; forms did not begin,
Only coming the moving of fluid sensation,
And pouring out laughing flowers,
A pensive wind, touching my soul,

"The end of longing…inside…,"
A penning, true, from my reservoir of sentiment,
Finding thoughtful awareness,
My mourning, my constancy in kneeling
At the feet of yesterday.

And I knew, for the moment of the dewdrop,
That I had, in the larger portion,
Made my prison, and in the small
Courage of vacillation, the agony of looking
And saying, of not looking and not saying,
I choose to remain there,
For life is more in contrast, the consort
Of pain giving over to small and grande
Fulfillment, his arm offered,
Once and more, to begin again.

Elizabeth
May 16, 2004
Early morning, awakening, breakfast with Bocelli,
The last line I had read in the past evening;

The stone of insight is heavy: I am pulled along
By my thought, and I cannot, now, take and lead.

Thoughts

Let me lie on a gentle peace,
Not one of angst and pressed fatigue,
But of putting down from steps
Of simple and good industries, as idyllic
Pastorals describe, of rose steps,
Golden steps whose leaving shadows glow
As silver below, reflecting
The eastern moonrise.
Let winds bring lullabies that only I can hear,
Because, perhaps, of the joy
Of yesterday's arms, the hands which
Touched today, the smiles that will
Announce, together, inside the glory of sunrise,
Of the promised morrow.

Let my back forget its straight leaning,
My shoulders to fold into softness,
And my arms and hands place in prayerful laying.

Cause ever, in these moments my head to bow,
Let the petals that cover the eyes of my thought,
But, more, of my heart, close into a moment's repose
And cleave to a sweet peace of a short,
Dark season where only friendly smoke and
Brilliant stars move in dance around
The maiden moon.
Her light not kept, but as chaste as
Her jeweled belt and as faithful key.

Elizabeth
January 4, 2007
Thoughts at the end of the day,
Resting in my bedroom

-And my pen brought swirls
And curls, and leaves that laughed
Out to me, out their imagined rainbow
Of greens; there came, too, presently,
A unicorn, with his majestic sprout,
Of myth, a rabbit, poised innocently,
Covered of furtive glance;
And an honorable hound, sitting,
Quietly in respectivity.

-And such brought a lightness,
A soft, if incomplete, content;
I was, as color comes,
Enjoying pause, in its expanding,
Full of brightened thought
And release in capturing –
Part of a cosem, a world that,
As the window attests,
Has come again, hateful, but good to me.

Elizabeth
October 24, 2004
After sketching part of a medieval motif
For painting, becoming tired

Even So —

The opiate of bruised lavender;
The lipsticked laughter
Of campari and soda;
The closing of mourning in twilight,
Beauty finding, in homesick hearts
Of seasonal passings;
Like ripples from a stone's throw,
Or echoes in memory –
More, haloes rising out of forgiveness,
Courage, and love –
The heart in achings, old, and nearer,
Reaches over and again
To catch the bark of deliverance,
Yet, even the grief which makes
Quick all that forgetting
Lays out in emptinesses.

Elizabeth
August 4, 2004
Unhappy moments, in my bedroom –
Fatigue with my own heart and its constant lack of oneness,
In any fashion; perhaps my appetite is consuming,
And makes unattractive all that I wish to give.
Nearing September, hauntingly beautiful September;
I think of Jim Whitehead_he would have liked this verse.
Surely the night would have perished part of me
Save one that spoke and touched,
Knowing my struggle, and bringing it to himself,
Dividing any pain so that my paints
Took on hues of beauty's meanings; and the antidote
Of word and color banished the hurting night,
I, then, escaping the Lazaretto, its calling
Perishing into now the content of nothing;
I, forgiven still again the cruel Venetian place,
Full into dark within the seed of struggling hope
When the ever miracle of awareness suddenly
Knows past the repose of cheek on folded arm_
Rest of fatigue in thought and movement,
And resolve to, again, will
And do feel and know.

Cycling: standing against the hard wind of words
And circumstance, and knowing all manner of beauty
In the place of its afterwards – until the next time –

Elizabeth
April 12, 2007
Following Dr. Norton's return call

Old Man Springtime

In daylight we find too often the flawed obvious,
Static and offensive (to the beauty we tenuously hold)
Inside unacceptable sound and movement;
In darkness we can find rarest beauty
In secrets which lift our soul,
Through living, pleasing movement, toward,
Even into, near spiritual meadows, those,
Found in morning, first,
Claire pure – altogether gathering a portion
Of the gift of love: old man, bringing again,
And again, new springtimes,
Reviewing rapture of a once time in its
Almost feeling of yesterday's brought image.

Elizabeth

What Are We

What are we about when we attempt – truly,
Earnestly, generously –
In the wrappings of humility and solitude –
Engaging in an honest conversation,
As we have ableness, with the divine portion
Of ourselves – we altogether, our purpose,
Our goal, yet in the manner of all who
Have dreamt the grail – spoken, of the
Unexplainable good, the aching in the heart
For a oneness of selves – to allow these separates
To come together so that the grace of unknown
Munificence – the lesser and more –
Be allowed to find and appropriate pattern,
A blending of spirits, divine and earthly,
Voice and word, consummation into
Holy consecration: - closeted prayer –
In the varieties that "closets" can be –

Elizabeth
February 2, 2015
Seeking, striving, in a kind of agony and hope for
The *"better strength…"* – *"in living well"* –
(*"strength"* – *"revenge"*) –
F. S. Fitzgerald
Twentieth century American novelist

Her Lady's Scarlet

The scarlet petunia of mid-summer,
Gathered, and pleasure to her mistress' eye,
Spread finally her fading fragrance
And form into silence, but in so,
Her passion, the delight of her lady,
Bore more strength than in her newness;
Every shade of crimson bled
Its path onto its ceramic dish:
Dying scarlet into shadowed magenta
With her essence of noir;
But it is the haute and the grande,
The sensual with the spiritual,
The, ultimately, epitome of the beautiful.

Elizabeth
July 27, 2009, midday
On consideration of the finality of mortal beauty:
A transitory suggestion with legion strength –
To remain a glimpse, a shadow, an image,
An idea which will not fade,
But be fondly passed to those following –

Beauty, of whatever fashion,
One of our many touches of immortality –

My fading petunia, in her beautiful capture
These days, growing into a kind of love –
Andso, my bittersweet lament –

Roseberries

And the night sang a mourning song,
Of hope lost, as are all my roseberries,
They departing while I knew
They were in such, perhaps partially
Veiled, farewelling.
But, found, Dear, found much,
Some roseberries, your kept kiss,
So that I know, as did the quieted touch,
To cry inside, to not, in simple ceremony,
Marry a moment into my spirit.
The roseberry of your voice
Is heavy whisper, the roseberries of strength,
Shoulders, an able wooden door,
And your laughter, its comfort and beauty,
Wielding the strength of a knight
In gold together with he of silver.

The stone buttress of resolve to find pattern
For your hand over mine,
Covering and drawing out my able,
Giving roseberry of many roseberry days
And their early waiting,
Generously embracing rose and wet
And receiving, in courage which had not
Needed contrasting against.

Oh Babe, ring out Thy roseberry need of me,
Joyful, very crimson vessels whose bellies reveal
That of red, that of warm:
Propers read make reverence,
Into berrysweet, berryholy, berryall.

And, in a good voice give in wishing,
To the unknown away; much of night to try –
On then out carry we, roseberries
Which grew up a soft mist,
Fragranced with softest rose,
Not ever to die, but only to die in faded
Strength, in all great resounding a good rosary
Can promise: propers read make for
Reverence, into berryweet,
Berryholy, berryall.

Andso, after you are gone away,
When you are again here,
We have not touched.
And the soprano of the cleaned night,
Mine, sing as heart's destiny –
The moment, masterful catcher of the colors
Of the roseberried, its Babe.

Oh Babe, if Thy roseberries
(were there truly, ever roseberries) –
Could be found, my reaching,
Copper-jeweled cup with the exquisite
Flowing of winter's silver,
Into summer's cloudsmoke,
How gently I would save, to allow my lips
(should roseberries continue this year and a day),
Wedding into moments there,
My passion unite of the now moment,
And roseberry moments of yesterday's
Roseberries remembered.

Elizabeth
Early spring, 2003, near Easter

I have no Thee to love me dear.

Elizabeth
Spring, 2019

And so, I watch you
Through your voice,
In your larger struggle,
But, too, in the roll call of smaller pathos;
And I love you in a kind of desperation,
Wishing that I could gather
The both of your soul
Into arms of just a small,
Comforting safety,
And that over and again.

Elizabeth
November 8, 2003

Could That...

Aberrant thought scapes have been
The whole of my wandering through tonight,
Today. I am alone in these scapes,
Knowing with a malevolent clarity of their sheep –
Like stance away from their apparently
Happy, conventional, even bourgeoise fellows.

Within these scapes, the sweet brings longing,
And the beautiful a mourning,
These caught up in the whispered smoke
Of knowing – that of tainting, apology, and conclusion.

Could laughter be full and round,
And not within the silence it bends to;
Could beauty satisfy in a singular purity
So that uneasy, uncertain wishes not begin
Their unfortunate taunting; could knowing,
Close after each poignant exchange,
And memory, die to its alternate curse –
Then burning candles would not be flowers
In flames, or the clock a dark sounding,
And love only love in, its all;
The antidotes of fervent prayer,
Embracing all that beautiful,
With words true – these bridges
To safety together imbue further,
Fuller antidotes of hope and trust,
Leaping out their secrets;
And my tender flowers, and golden,
Of innocent good.

Elizabeth
October 4, 2004

Not a good day but grateful to be able
To think in mostly reasonable fashion – trying still, still
Driving in late afternoon light,
The shadow of a street sign was passed through,
Its contours and hues of bright and dark
Finding somehow a beauty,
A softening, a playful presence
In its pasture of stone and heat.

In the moment, it quite ran away,
However, capturing on my vehicle,
And within an inside and backward glance,
Found just as quickly to rearrange,
To the permission of the sun_
Into larger, dimming, shadow and dark.

The visage in radiant greeting,
The hand in generous touch;
The voice in song – a very – rapture –
In a kind of hallowed acceptance,
The existential altering, backwards,
Toward, again a more impatient soul,
So was the moment passed,
Within and beyond.

I feel deeply always,
But especially when I am "high,"
But I cannot hold on to these tastes
Of plentiful soul,
Even that of momentarily arranging paradise;
And if left to feel, then, darkened and lonely.

Elizabeth
July 14, 2004
Near daybreak
Countyline Road in the late afternoon, yesterday

Forgiving the Day
the sacrament of acceptance

Solitude offers immeasurable wealth, pensive
And peaceful hours which allow reviews
And excursions, together with sparrings into positive
Avenues of healthy acceptance, as with the disparity
Of entering dissonance.
The moth or thief does not take these gifts,
For when viewing garden aesthetics,
In their decline, having enjoyed
True bliss in this bounty of beauty –
When the eye allows the image of spirit in death –
As lovely as that in life –
Its hues only of a different realm:
The time is to pause, to forgive the day,
The phenomenon of awareness.
And when the task,

The wager of will and circumstance,
Cannot, will not, - yet must to bend
To lost will, in circumstance –
Physical feats, admirable and not –
There is pause for true forgiveness
Of the hour, the day.
In sweetness, more, in contentment, celestial,
When spent with the day's importances so that the
"little death" presses –
When all efforts to gather thought,
Express silences of the heart, with their artful
Messages – or to again offer sayings in instances
Of the caesura of timelessness –
When natural laws converge and our needs must know –
There is a consenting – more, a trusting,
A pause of true forgiveness of the day.
Whether serf or lord,
Within a hut, alone, or a fiefdom,
Wide, perhaps we should know the necessity
Of the quietening of our consciousness;
From words on the wind;
From the effervescing dew;
From piercing sunlight's gold – in our
Ebbing strength or our need to bow in obeisance.
_Good, perhaps, to let our solitudes pull aside
The drape of individuation,
Of pride,
And strengthen
Our fealty, our honor,
Our fullest devotion,
To absolutely ensue,
To our own,
The formidable gift
Of grace,
The wait of faith,
Into its ceremonial
Wealth.

Elizabeth
November 3 , 2016
Just at bedtime

Closing Hours

In these most distant corners of the day,
Near the hour of the midnight Rose,
Reflection fills the boulevards of thought,
And comes again a weighing of steps,
Musings of their little importances, their worth,
Or less, the distance behind and forward.
In evaluation bares a lessening, and, on good
Occasion a glimpse of glory;
Ah – so lovely the matter of choice,
So exacting that of circumstance, but,
In a kind of radiance, we find our own,
Our self, to move, through lighted
Haloes of knowing and feeling,
The sterling power of reason with sentiment.

Elizabeth
The first two weeks of November, 2016

Let me weep to Thee, my gratitude,
And pen my thoughts of praise;
And let me know inside myself that solitude
With Thee, sit a royal family to my need.
Let then, worthy be my presence to the feast,
And with joyful spirit let me embrace all
Moments given invitation to Thy provided table.

Elizabeth
November 11, 2016
Eveningtime

Bittersweet Glory

Within the bittersweet shadows
That clothe the evening skies of late September,
Our hearts turn into a pale rose,
With forgotten petals, and fainting breath.
The radiance that it once was
Suggests to our soul to look backwards,
To its days of fullest glory,
But the sweetness in its death
Chides this thought so that the last image
Will live, the giving,
Not more than the glory,
But as much, and, at the last.

Elizabeth
September 20, 2018
Eventide

Truest Sentiment

A woman's love, with its giving,
Is its most true,
Even into perishing,
And uniquely golden,
It, yet, if left her heart,
The treasure,
Alone.

Elizabeth
May 24, 2018
With early coffee and tender thoughts

O God, our help in ages past,
Our hope in years to come…

"Mighty God"
Of Chad

Oh Ye Gods...

Oh ye gods, whose ancient rooms
Read of fabled glory,
Whose arms do battle with fierce winds,
And bathe in delicate movings;
Who pour freely the sweetness of golden nectar –
Speak to me your wisdom of warmth:
How does my heart fill, so ably,
Full with love, so close to the wind,
To the nectar; and yet,
In sweetest pain, fall so much
The distance, as to be unable to love.

Elizabeth
The eve of another Christmas Eve, alone,
Holding my other hand with its only other
2016

The sinews of your flesh,
The blood drops of your soul –
This issue of life out your heart's cleavage –
These somehow transmute into the coins of
Wealthy pain which purchase, once again,
Your leften self, demoralized,
But in the break,
In the smoke of its agony –
Out of these reaches go out to new joy in,
Again, being.

Elizabeth
-How – 2016, near midnight
December 23 –

-my plume, my faithful plume-
Music to the side –

All That I Have Spoken...

All that I have spoken with voice,
Pen and moving brush –
Or any other expressive means,
Provides a beautifully simple, yet also
Complex truth, if only for me:
Every dream, awake, asleep, its image,
Thought and sentiment clothing,
I have experienced, here, in this cosmos,
Either in reality-based consciousness
Or in some form of knowing beyond,
Beside the known ordinary.
My words and expressions, any such
"out of me" are records that I hold to,
That I dream of re-visiting, however long,
Or full, or difficult the provided path of dust –
Or perhaps an uncharted walk with
New impressions as I move,
Perhaps in marvelous Ulysses light.
These kept expressions\experiences will
Be my strength, until consummation,
Of the mystic all, ever –
For they are stored in my heart,
And the heart does not forget.

Elizabeth
November 24, 2018
Saturday afternoon, after Thanksgiving
Reference to Ulysses is from Tennyson's verse
Of the fabled warrior.
The tortuous quiet in solitude,
Yet ordained of peace,
With gentle fingers, labors
Toward soothing woundings
And weariness of responding.
Still, in the tender fingers, their reaching,
Rests no accompaniment of voice,
Or step, yet smile or touch.

If there could be a garden in some
Distant corner which houses a heart
With these knowings,
Then I would find my peace in quiet oneness,

To be alone in togetherness,
To know spirit bound
Into truest freedom.

Elizabeth
July 31, 2006
Thoughts, early Sunday morning,
On choosing, with resolve, but unhappily,
To remain alone.
Remnants of J. Donne, an old, but evolving theme

Why am I, and who;
A lovely rind being held,
Suspended as a pale between awareness
And fullest night,
Until it has no more semblance
To life and light.
And where does the spent rind rest,
And with what knowing:
My raven with Dot's gold;
Unknowing as fair as knowing,
The path with steps laid over by still others,
So that thoughts and sighs
Gather to my pen,
Unable to answer why or who I am.
And the dark answers –
Ever stillness.

Elizabeth
August 3, 2004
Nine-thirty pm

To Die the Day

It is difficult to die the day,
When the feast served has been
Sumptuous – heavy and sweet.
To close a good is to fear,
That the repeat will be not to follow,
For angels and dragons have their turns.
It is difficult to die the day for reminders
Gather to manifest anew, but never again to be –
The loss into never, irredeemable:
The dew fall, the petal;
The uniquely exquisite, today's sunset.
It is difficult to die the day for it foretells
The fuller harvest – the final grasses to become brown,
Most to be interned into their source,
The ever earth; and the seeds,
Decayed in their lost usefulness –
Fruits, their jewel-like freshness into the deep,
Wounded purple and dark of decay –
Either hanging still, in hope,
Or fallen to the downward into their dark
Of endless night.
Ought but the vastness of the carnage of all we know
And love is that it be strewn into the sunrise
That will restore, all –
But a retelling, not a once true –
If we could know, and understand.

Elizabeth
September 3, 2015
-somber thoughts tonight, following a difficult day-

Ah, Morpheus, visit me
With a long, sweet draught
Which will take all but the pleasurable
Ambiance of lavender, resting,
Yet, of rainfall, gentle, still;
Of the hour that flies, but leaving
Those ever young, of the giving in love,
Of my heart, alone –
Accepted, enough.

Elizabeth

January 18, 2004
J. on my heart, all day,
So difficult, sometimes –

In a hurried moment, I was
Miraculously aware and presence
Stood silently by in the faithful
Lamplight which reached out
And touched the mystic lady
Of my thought.
Again, and once again,
I had passed through another
"little death."

Elizabeth
February 15, 2004

"I do not remember when I first saw you,
Or was aware of who you are;
It is just that my first knowing of you,
As you are,
And to me,
Was a metaphorical image:
You were, in your all,
As red flame, and I knew
That I wanted to go toward it."

Elizabeth
December 26, 2017

Love is, in our most,
A beautiful morning game,
A terrific sparring of wills;
Secrets and disclosure, with gentle,
And those of agoneyed strength;
Its, still, secrets; pressings, and releasings,
And for us, most, we come
To wish fresh water,
In passions storm of winds.

The day is, now, in apology
After the noon hour,
And silver lights in the heavens
Suggest a sterile cold.

The clock need, then, send no message
Of the hour, for tense is fluid
And is always flowing into those
Portions that lie in the away.

Time held is awkward to its offspring
And brother, the present,
And time, stilled,
Is death to all that it
Attended and dressed.

Elizabeth
October 14, 2004
Cycle down, very deep, especially now at twilight;
I am yet alone, God's child, alone.

Four Images

Among flowers, there is always a dark rose,
Beneath, a subtle blasphemy,
One not open to the quickly moving eye,
But to the eye, to whom having come
The unforgiving shroud of hesitation,
Is brought thoughtful,
And in tenses select, without its own
Pardon effecting the stumbling eye,
That of increasing mortal wisdom.

His kiss, to my open palm,
Certain premonition of dark,
But in the moment, new and softly lighted,
Our eager, discovering passion;
Early – a lost response, and as the meadow
In spring, forgotten;
And of those offerings remaining,
Only a reflection of that first radiance,
Even an hour of glory.

Blackberry blossoms, politely arranging
Within the morning's sunlight,
Dancing among thistle and briar,
On roadsides, still, their promise,
A happy wager to the children who sleep
In my heart, awakened yet another Easter,
Pastels and new warmth embracing
My waiting need,
Wrapping it in arms that
Can reach only from yesterday.

Elizabeth
Easter Eve 2001
The fourth image cannot, just now, be found

Of Import

Titles and robes are of little import –
More, soundings out fresh laughter
Of the blackberry woman;
Melodies which are softened and smoothed
By falling onto holy serge
Sewed into the habit;
Aged fish and cabbage that dress small wisdom,
Or, perhaps, the just arrived lady,
Strong, her sash of purist gold,
Midst jeweled lace –
Of import, words of these, sounds
Enlarging sweet whispers, and sighs –
Echoes distant in wisdom;
And still, blessings passing with intentioned steps –
These all stand monument to he who receives them,
After time, and past appraisal –
These ought unto no greater good,
To the deserving in their hearing,
Their catching, their holding.

Elizabeth
August 14, 2015

So much is lost to the moment,
Yet how beautifully they hang,
As flowing rich tapestry
In soft hours between sleep
And wakefulness,
The wanting, wayfaring heart
Ever seeking.

How gold the gold, how dim to cover
So as not to hurt in its passing.

Elizabeth
August 25, 2005

…and together with the exquisite yellow
Of duet honeysuckle,
May this blessing fill thy soul with peace and truth,
The very gold of love,
Both select and rare:
Gathering toward thee now,
My adagio of hope.

Elizabeth
March 26, 2004

When I am close to the riddle, it is even
Partially unraveling; I am in,
Yet, a desert, where, as charred fruit,
All has been, and all is, then,
Dry dust, dark cinder jewels –
Except my insisting unseen –
But to my soul which has found,
Metaphorically, release –
Etchings, left in my imagined,
But in sentiment, truthful drama,
Of individual pathos,
Not at all, in humanity's scene,
Alone, but mine alone:
Ought but sweet memory, brought
Down on the rains of time, left, and, alone.

Elizabeth
August 2002
Saddened, confused in reporting my most real feelings;
This a time of uselessness and great void, but truly alone.
Oh flower of knowing, open yet wide to me,
Letting the center hold more than dreams
And promises have said,
More than the whole of the wisdom
In the eyes of all Abrahams.

Elizabeth

Given to me, then, was a gift I cannot
Have in waking hours, but the ever
Clever, and today, kindly,
Yearning keeper of my heart
Was accepted by my thought;
And I have memory of all of Thee,
Thee resplendent only unto me,
And I, with their beauty,
Queenly radiant.

Elizabeth
October 7, 2005

"And I am left..."

The most worthy, endless circle that lies in the
Path of existence touches me with
Amazement, over, and over again:
As often as day and night are,
The exuberance and hope of morning,
The stoic will of endurance in a day,
The resignation and acceptance in evening and night,
With its ever-promised spectacle of new day –
Over and over again, within the trappings of mood,
Disappointment, fatigue, and beleaguered hope –
On, on, to more of the pattern to be played out.
We mortals, lesser gods,
Die, but rest immortal that we do,
For a season, on these *"golden,*
Earthly sands" – continue.

Elizabeth
2009

Flower my voice and the contours of my face,
That my gathering be the berry full,
And of passionate hue granted.
And good could have left its holding
Theory, eloquent: cast aside,
To in love be loved,
A becoming of threads that,
As evening vespers, bind into righteousness,
Faithfulness, and speaking wisdoms,
Elegant and grey, these,
Together, declaring the shadowed fable of truth.

Elizabeth
June 9, 2001

Can we be loved for the roses we grow,
Brought into tender sentiment for the tears
Caught by our watch;
Touched in thought for the stones we lift away,
Blessed for seeing inside the deep of another.

If so, then let me be alive, awake,
To caress the earth,
Reach for falling dark awarenesses,
Lift away weights too heavy for others'
Given strength, open my soul to the universe
Of all knowing and unknowing –
For in these beatitudes I find a self,
One that I as flowered companionable,
Gentle with the hours,
And comforting when seasons close.

Elizabeth
2007

Conclusion

If then, we wish to enlarge and grow, we must stretch, and bend, yet also undergo pruning. We are closer, then, to the realization of our whole selves, and this circumstance is, in part, a dark journey through the oftentimes difficult rooms, "behind", and within. Every excursion does not effect a rose, but a rose does redeem the genuine effort of the heart that continues to seek.

As has been presented, the hinterlands can be established, as is night, unseen except when investigated, a reservoir of knowledge, often despair, but often peace. We approach it, in its certainty through thought, although ambiances can add unto.

We can still seek that we do not know, review the unimaginative; we can attend all in current, social reasoning – the absurd, the unbalanced, the illogical – and we can give moments to the comforting reasonable. We can gather to us, finding hope and clarity to matters which require "time," quiet organization, review, the seemingly impossible so that special heights in learning and behavior are possible – and we can recognize levels of knowing quite outside scientific theory, the I – Thou relationship being given attention.

"Hope is the forward appendage of thought;" with these together, we learn the two dimensions of truth: trust and fear; these render one safe in knowing, being dependent on self-appraisal. We know, finally, that we often must go into darkness to learn and leave it to live the respite, having always the courage to touch a star, an awakening paradox known, perhaps, only to humans – *"for man is the only animal who knows that one day he will die."*

– only enough light to stave off the last, smallest dragon, old Chanticleer, himself: to then in the announced light – discover the come rose –– the ever recipe:

Recognition
Acquiescing
Acceptance
Resignation
Hope

Andso, "we do not do the best we can; we only do all that we can. – oh, Mamma …
– the ever true –

Concluding Quote

"Whether we realize it or not,
Simply to be human
Is to long for release from mundane existence,
With its confining walls
Of finitude and mortality."

Huston Smith
"Why Religion Matters"